WHERE I COME FROM

WHERE I
COME FROM

Stories from the Deep South

RICK BRAGG

ALFRED A. KNOPF · NEW YORK · 2020

THIS IS A BORZOI BOOK
PUBLISHED BY ALFRED A. KNOPF

Copyright © 2020 by Rick Bragg

All rights reserved. Published in the United States by Alfred A. Knopf,
a division of Penguin Random House LLC, New York, and
distributed in Canada by Penguin Random House Canada Limited, Toronto.

www.aaknopf.com

Knopf, Borzoi Books, and the colophon
are registered trademarks of Penguin Random House LLC.

Library of Congress Cataloging-in-Publication Data
Names: Bragg, Rick, author.
Title: Where I come from : stories from the deep South / Rick Bragg.
Other titles: Stories from the deep South
Description: First edition. | New York : Alfred A. Knopf, 2020.
Identifiers: LCCN 2020005021 (print) | LCCN 2020005022 (ebook) |
ISBN 9780593317785 (hardcover) | ISBN 9780593317792 (ebook)
Subjects: LCSH: Southern States—Social life and customs—Anecdotes | Southern
States—Biography—Anecdotes
Classification: LCC F209.6 .B733 2020 (print) | LCC F209.6 (ebook) | DDC 975—dc23
LC record available at https://lccn.loc.gov/2020005021
LC ebook record available at https://lccn.loc.gov/2020005022

Jacket images: (truck) Owaki / Kulla / Getty Images;
(goat) Science Photo Library/Getty Images
Jacket design by Jenny Carrow

Manufactured in Canada
First Edition

For Jo, and John

Contents

Contents

Contents

Contents

WHERE I COME FROM

Jo

~⁓

I AM HER SISTER'S BOY, so she read every word I ever wrote. And every word was perfect, even the clumsy or purple ones, the double negatives and dangling participles and run-on sentences that galloped, comma after comma, across the page. But still perfect. I know because Aunt Jo called, after every story, after every chapter in every book, to tell me so.

I knew, with her, I had a ringer, at least one reader who would tell me it was good, and she was proud of me. Everybody needs a ringer, in this racket, and I will miss her so.

She passed away in the fall. I forget, sometimes, that she is gone, and when the phone rings I still wonder, for a moment, if it is her.

I do not really believe in ghosts, not the way some writers do, down here. Still, if you read these stories and you have something bad to say, I would keep it to myself.

The stories in this collection are of the South's gentler, easier nature. It is a litany of great talkers, blue-green waters, deep casseroles, kitchen-sink permanents, lying fishermen, haunted mansions, and dogs that never die, things that make this place more than a dotted line on a map or a long-ago failed rebellion, even if only in some cold-weather dream.

It is the best of us, I believe. My Aunt Jo was the best of it, too, and so belongs at its very beginning. She *was* the South, in so many ways. In an age when the South seems full of posers, she was bona fide.

She won her first turkey roasting pan in a raffle run by a guy named Popcorn at a filling station on Alabama 21, in a time when WALLACE stickers were still turning from an angry blue and pink to a sad, faded gray.

She made peanut butter sheet cakes for fifty years, to celebrate our birthdays. If you lined them up they would stretch all the way to Montgomery. Every July 26, she put a twenty-dollar bill in a birthday card, and sent it to me in the mail. I got one for my sixtieth birthday.

I added it up. Over a lifetime, I could have bought a used car.

In this time of clichés, she was a revival, a Tupperware party, as genuine as dinner on the ground. She loved Elvis, and Jesus, and Uncle John, but could be iron-headed and lock-jawed if you made her mad, though sometimes it was hard to figure out what you did or said to make her that way. It was just her prerogative, as a Southern lady.

She was not the veranda South, the cotillion South, only the South I write about most, the one a person can love without qualification or reservation, without having to explain your damn self. She was not the South of meanness and small-mindedness, not the political South that yearns to turn back time. She was uninterested in waving anyone's battle flag, in being part of anyone's club or society, though she did work for the U.S. Postal Service while her husband was up in South Carolina as a young PFC.

In her obit photo, she poses against a 1955 Chevrolet in a pair of what we used to call pedal pushers, framed by a field of cotton, a tall pine, and a red-dirt hill. It was taken in '59, the year she married, the year I was born.

She is smiling, and why not? Uncle John raced that car at the

Green Valley Dragway, and blew their doors off. They were paying on a little wood-frame Jim Walter Home, and dined on good foot-long chili dogs at Pee Wee Johnson's place on the Fridays he got paid. As she got older she wore cat's-eye glasses, and took my momma to buy groceries on Friday at the A&P. They always got Green Stamps.

Like most Southerners in old age, she was perhaps most comfortable in the past, but not in a search for some doomed ideal. She opened her photo albums and drifted back in time, touching on the people she loved like a child tapping a picket fence with a stick. She talked to my momma every night at nine, and over the years it became the official end of the day; everything after that was leaning toward tomorrow. She and my uncle never had children of their own, and never had a day without them.

You probably had one just like her. She was that woman you see in the grocery store or the Walmart or restaurants, the one that people my age say of, as they go by: "You know, she helped raise me."

And they all but bow their heads when they say it. It might be a grandmother, or a godmother, or just the old woman down the road, who watched over them, one eye on *As the World Turns* as they pushed a toy truck across her linoleum floor, one shoe off, apple sauce on their jumper, and crackers in their hair.

Their names became shorthand for an unsecured loan on date night, or a last-minute haircut in the kitchen, so we would not go out into the world looking like a Philistine.

Blood was everything. She forgave us, my brothers and me, almost every stupid thing we ever did, yet would not have cable TV in her house, because of the wickedness therein.

She died with me owing her about two thousand dollars, in hamburger money alone.

I saw my Uncle John the other day. He had yet to move her

slippers from their place in front of the sofa. A few days later, he passed away in his sleep. Their's being a Southern story, it could not have happened any other way.

The house is filled with their history, and mine. There is a thin layer of dust on the books and magazines that hold my work, piled in front of the television. And I wonder sometimes if they will just come tumbling down, someday, an avalanche of words, every one of them approved, or blessed, by my Aunt Jo.

This book is not intended to be a cold-blooded examination of the South, but it is not all harps and flowers, either. It touches, now and then, on a South that breaks our hearts. But, as I said, it is mostly the better part of us, which is easier to do, unless you are counting tombstones. I also understand that some of these things I consider to be the purvey of the South exist outside our borders; I know you can find them even in places where people fish through the ice, and salt their city streets and their Cream of Wheat. Somewhere, in Fargo, even, I bet an Aunt Jo is helping to raise somebody like me. Maybe they are just American stories, and this just happens to be where I come from. I am a Southern writer, by birth. My Aunt Jo said so.

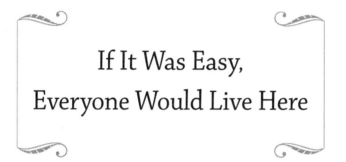

If It Was Easy,
Everyone Would Live Here

The Outcast

I SHOULD HAVE GIVEN UP, I suppose, after the goat.
He was not a regular goat. He was more part goat, part rhinoceros, about the size of a small horse, but with devil horns. He looked out on the world through spooky yellow eyes, and smelled like . . . well, I do not have the words to say. My little brother, Mark, bought him at the sprawling trade day in Collinsville, Alabama, for seventy-five dollars; I would have given him a hundred not to. The first thing the creature did, after coming into our possession, was butt the side of a truck. You have to be one terror of a goat to assault a Ford. His name, my little brother said, was Ramrod.

"Why would you buy such a thing?" I asked my brother. He told me he planned to purchase a bunch of nanny goats to "get with" Ramrod, after whatever courtship it was that goats required. Ramrod would beget little Ramrods, who would beget more, till the whole world was covered in ill-tempered mutant goats. I think, sometimes, we did not love that boy enough.

Ramrod moved into his new home in a beautiful mountain pasture in northeastern Alabama, and, first thing, butted heads with my mother's equally ill-tempered donkey, Buckaroo. Buck staggered a few steps, and his head wobbled drunkenly from side to side, but he did not fall unconscious. This, in Buck's mind, constituted a victory, and he trotted off, snorting and blowing, like he was somebody.

My point is, Ramrod was a goat not to be messed with.

Later that year, I was fishing with my brothers in the stock pond in that same pasture. The water was mostly clear, and you could see the bream in the shallows and the dark shapes of bass in the deeper end. For a change, even I was catching fish and pulled in a few nice little bass. My cast, to me, was immaculate, my aim perfect, my mechanics sound, especially for the clunky crankbait I was throwing.

"But I'm not gettin' much distance," I complained to my big brother, Sam.

"It's fine," he said, and with an easy flick of his wrist sent a black rubber worm sailing beyond my best cast of the day.

I decided to put a little more mustard on it. I let my lure dangle about a foot and a half from the tip of the rod, reared back, torqued, and started forward with a powerful heave . . . and hooked Ramrod, who had crept up behind me to do me some kind of grievous harm, right between his horns.

Ramrod, who for perhaps the first time in his long life seemed unsure of what to do, took off running. My drag, which was not set for a goat of any size, sang.

Sam, who has never been too surprised by anything in his whole laconic, irritating life, gazed at the retreating goat as if this were a thing he witnessed every single day.

"Can't remember if that was a ten-pound test I put on that baitcaster," he said, as if it made a difference. "You can't catch no fish with heavy line. They can see it," and he made another cast.

The goat ran on. I considered, briefly, just standing my ground and trying to reel him in, to play him like a great tarpon, or a marlin. Instead, I began to run parallel with him, reeling in the slack as I did, as I have seen great anglers do with giant fish on the TV.

I guess I thought I could eventually get close enough to reach out and snatch the hook out of his head. I truly did not want to hurt him, but that was foolish, of course; you could not hurt Ramrod with a hammer or hand grenade.

As it turned out, the point of the hook, not even to the barb, had snagged in the bony base of one horn, and the crankbait jangled atop his head. He was not wounded; he was just mad. He quit running about the time I ran out of line, and my little brother, who had a sort of telepathic bond with this creature, calmly walked over and pulled the hook free while the goat stood there like a pet. Then he and the goat both gave me a dirty look, as if hooking him were something I woke up that morning intending to do.

I went back to the pond, frazzled, and—I am not kidding—immediately hooked a water oak, a blackberry bush, and a low-slung power line. There are witnesses to this. I shuffled off with a rubber worm dangling high above me; it was Cherokee Electric's problem now. I was done fishing that day, and seriously considered being done for good. I walked to the house defeated, but not ashamed, at least as far as Ramrod was concerned. That goat never liked me, anyhow.

This is a true story. Great anglers, the kind who tie their own flies and read the tides and have fished the deep blue for leviathans, will most likely shake their sun-bronzed heads in pity and sad wonder over this. But the bad fishermen out there—you know who you are—will merely nod in understanding and sympathy and, I hope, some degree of solidarity. The only reason they have not caught a goat is that, so far, one has not made their acquaintance, or wandered into the proximity of their backswing.

But perhaps the worst thing about it is that the best fisherman I know, my brother Sam, did not even think that, in the long, sad epic of my fishing life, this episode was remarkable at all. He did not even *tell* it to anyone, not in the decade since. To him, it was just the kind of thing a poor fisherman like me was likely to do, was somehow fated or destined to do, assuming of course that he did not, first, fall out of a boat and drown.

"What is it, truly," I asked, "I do wrong?" He was too kind to give voice to it.

He just spread his hands, palms up, as if to say: *Everything.* The proof hangs on the wall of the garage, row after row of tangled, rusty, and forever abandoned rods and reels, some of them hopelessly entangled with others. One day, with my toolbox and a bottle of good oil, I'll resurrect them, or try. I've caught my big brother staring at them with the saddest look on his face. He used to fix them himself, till it dawned on him it was a thing without hope, or end.

I remember the first good fish I ever caught, the first one I was proud of, and it made me, for good and bad, a fisherman the rest of my life. I remember, most clearly, my bait, a knot of red worms in a clump of topsoil that was at least part cow manure. I kept them in a discarded blue plastic margarine tub that I had carefully, scientifically aerated, using a hammer and a nail to poke holes in the snap-on lid.

I was maybe seven years old, perched on a slab of rock by a jade-colored slow-moving creek that was easing toward the Coosa. I cast into the deep pools with a closed-face Zebco 202, not catching a thing at first, just loving the motion of it, and the peace it seemed to create inside my mind even then.

The sunlight was losing its battle with the thick trees, and I knew I had to be getting home soon; then, I felt that hard pull on the line. I did not have to set the hook, but I pretended to, to look like a big boy, and reeled in a pretty little bass, just a pound or so, even allowing for the inevitable lie. For a few fine seconds, I just looked at it—the color, the pattern on its scales—and as I worked the hook free, it did what fish do, and as it squirmed, I hooked myself in the thumb.

I let the fish go, and a kindly old drunk man fishing upstream shakily but carefully unsnagged the hook, which had not gone in past the barb, from my thumb. I wailed.

"Hush," he said. "You ain't kilt."

And while it hurt like hell, I knew, even then, two true and perfect things. One, that I was bad at this, to the point of wounding myself, routinely.

Two, that it was a swap I was willing to make.

I know that I am not alone in this frailty, because I have heard other fishermen also lay claim to the title of worst fisherman in the world, since there is little point in being the second- or third-worst fisherman in the world. If you are going to be miserable at something, you might as well get a plaque for it.

You would think we would be too ashamed of our ineptitude to talk about it much, but there is a balm in knowing you are not alone, I guess in the same way addicts find solace in a circle of chairs and the company of the likewise afflicted. I guess we should all just line up on a creek bank, and confess: "Hello, my name is so-and-so, and I am a fisherman and I suck."

Then, we would all file over to the snack table for Vienna sausages, saltines, and beanie weenies. I would be sure to invite my friend, the fine writer Sonny Brewer, who once looked me right in the eye and said: "I have never caught a fish."

It took a man to say that. He has caught one in the ten years since.

But there is a special shame in this, for me. I was born to anglers. My great-grandfather fished for survival during Reconstruction. In the Great Depression, my grandfather pulled jack salmon from the water and slipped them in his coat pockets, and once lifted a massive, mean snapping turtle from the Coosa with his bare hands. Both my brothers catch fish. My big brother is almost a Zen master at it; he worked second shift at the cotton mill and fished bass tournaments at dawn, almost always finishing in the money and winning more than a few. My mother considered a rod and reel to be cheating, and used a cane pole to snatch a million bream from the ponds and creeks and backwater; she knew from looking at the sky if there would be fish for supper, and seasoned her cornmeal and set it aside before she walked to the water. She fished with red worms she gathered from under rotten logs; she never bought a worm in her life.

A man who could not fish was pitiful. Such men rode around without a spare tire, did not even own a toolbox or a pair of work boots, and got squeamish if they had to pull a tick off a dog. Well, my spare is aired up, and I have never seen a tick I wouldn't pull. But as a fisherman, I am just missing something, something that is both mechanical and mystical and, I am sorry to say, apparently permanent.

It dawned on me, only in middle age, that as many times as I have fished with my big brother, it was never once in a tournament, never once when there was money on the line.

"You just don't know how to feel," my brother said.

I thought for a moment he was trying to be sensitive, but he was being technical.

"Look," he said. "If you put some sticks, and rocks, and other stuff in a bucket, and you reach your hand in that bucket and feel around, you can tell, by feel, the sticks from the rocks, and all the rest of it, even if I hold it so you can't see inside it. When you fish, you can't touch the bottom, what's under there, so you got to feel through your line, feel it when your bait slides across a rock, or almost gets snagged in sticks and brush and stuff, and feel it, 'specially, when he bumps that bait, and when he takes it. You got to feel all the difference in all of that, or you spend all your time gettin' hung up, or you let the fish get off, or let him spit out that bait. You don't feel it."

He was not being unkind.

"You hadn't fished enough, and you hadn't fished when you had to, like Grandpa and them did, and I did. We *had* to catch fish. They had to fish to eat, and I had to fish good to pay for my gas, and for the entry fee. I can think of one time, maybe, that I didn't weigh in enough to pay my entry fee, and my gas.

"You fish for fun. You don't have to *ketch*."

He had a point. I remember, a hundred years ago, fishing for crappie from Aunt Edna's houseboat, and dozing off. I didn't wake, even when a big crappie swallowed my minnow and began to pull.

My cousins would take the rod from my hands and reel it in, then put it back. "Anything else?" I asked my brother.

"Bird's nests."

"What?"

"When you cast, you almost always make a bird's nest," he said.

"Not every time," I said.

"Almost," he said. "You spend all your time . . . well, the truth is that *I* spend all *my* time trying to get that bird's nest out of your reel, so you can cast again."

"I can drop a rubber worm in a five-gallon bucket twenty yards away . . . if there ain't no blackberry bushes in the way, or tree limbs, or power lines," I said.

"Till you make a bird's nest," he said. "You have to know exactly when you want that bait to drop, and where, and feel it as that line runs out, and . . ."

"Then why do you fish with me?" I asked. He did not dignify that with an answer.

He is my big brother. I will always be his little brother. Little brothers are chuckleheads.

But a lot of days, a whole lot of good days, there is no money on it.

Please understand that I have caught a lot of fish, in freshwater, in brackish bays, and in salt. I have filled coolers with delicious speckled trout, red snapper, and more, and turned loose big bass with a never-ending sense of wonder. I've fished in the Keys, and off Miami, and off a pier in Puerto Rico on a long night, when it seemed like I was the only man for an ocean or more. There are times when I think the best moments of my life have been filled, one cast at a time, on the flats of Tampa Bay. If there is a more beautiful sight than a speck almost as long as your arm cutting through that water to take the bait, I do not know it. A Spanish mackerel, nose to tail, is a work of art. Fishing is the one thing I will get out of bed for in early morning . . . well, that and biscuits and gravy.

But it just seems that, almost always, if there was a boat involved, or a hook, I could turn it into a dark comedy. On an alligator hunt in Lake Okeechobee, which is fishing of an altogether different reality, I miscalculated a leap from one boat to another in the middle of the deep rim canal and damn near drowned in the pitch dark with the red eyes of the alligators glowing all around me.

After a good day of fishing in Mobile Bay, I injured myself not in the boat but in a terrible fish-cleaning accident. I did not cut myself; I backed up without looking and fell over a tree stump.

In the Gulf of Mexico, in hundred-degree heat, I almost killed myself cranking in what had to be a record-setting red snapper only to land its lower lip . . . just a lip. My shipmates said it must have been a shark. I think I jerked its lip off, from sheer brute force, but have since been hooted down.

On another trip, sick of being cooked to a deep red by the Alabama sun, I bought a fine broad-brimmed hat.

"That is a lady's hat," said my fishing buddy.

"Shut up," I said. But when no one was looking, I checked inside the rim for the label. Damn.

There is a phenomenon on the shores of Mobile Bay called the jubilee, when a drop in the oxygen levels in the water, I am told, causes flounder, crabs, and other marine life to swarm to shallow waters, practically beaching themselves, and people along the shore rush among them with baskets and buckets and nets. Even I could catch a fish there, if someone would just loan me a bucket.

But it has never been truly about the catching. I love fishing, but sometimes, if I would admit it, I love more the idea of fishing, of being on the water or just at the lip of the pond, and the glide of a pelican, or the clean smell, upwind of the outboard motor.

"I think fish are beautiful," I let slip once to a real fisherman, Skip Jones, who grew up on Mobile Bay.

I will always appreciate his answer. "I do, too," he said.

So the difference is merely in the catching, and I guess I'd rather be a bad fisherman, or a fake one, than no fisherman at all. I remember, once, watching a big ol' boy fling his cast net into the bay for baitfish. The clumsy-looking wad of net fanned out gracefully into the water and came up shining with silver. I tried it, and it landed in a wad and came up empty, though I might have knocked a few baitfish out as I hurled it into the water. But you can buy bait, and you can, from time to time, get lucky, because even a bad fisherman snags something now and then. It really does not have to happen all that much, to feed the idea, and make me a fisherman, more or less.

You Ain't Goin' Nowhere

~⌒

I HAVE SOMETIMES BEEN LUCKY IN LIFE, dancing between raindrops, falling into the septic tank only to come out smelling like, if not roses, at least not a septic tank. You can't count on luck, but in my experience, like the proverbial blind hog, I always seemed to stumble on a fat acorn now and then. I do not expect it to be that way forever; I suspect I have about used mine up.

But seldom, I thought as I waited in line at the Birmingham airport, had I blundered into luck like this. I had received a call from nice people asking if I would do a brief talk in Hawaii, for actual money, with free first-class airfare. In January. Now, January in the Deep South is not like what they have in Wisconsin, but that particular winter we had a rare cold spell. The weatherman warned us to bring in the dogs and wrap the pipes.

"Bring it on," I smirked. As the Southland froze, I'd be going tubular on an emerald-colored wave in the Pacific, waving at the wahines as I glided onto the sand, where someone, I'm certain, would hang flowers around my neck and hand me a coconut filled with a fruity rum drink.

"Aloha," they would say.

"Aloha, your own self," I'd reply.

Like most people in my zip code, I learned most of what I know about the islands from watching Elvis in *Blue Hawaii* at the Midway Drive-In. I do not actually surf, have never seen a wahine or even learned exactly what that means, and don't drink much. But who knew what I would do when I got there? It was a magical land, far away. I could be a surfer, or a sot. I could be Elvis. We are kin to him, on my grandma's side.

I stood there in the security line, dreaming about luaus and sizzling roasted pork and volcanos spewing red into the tropical sky. I think I heard, faintly, a ukulele play.

I rushed to the gate.

"The flight's canceled," the gate agent said.

"I shall rebook," I said.

She told me the connections did not look good. You do not actually fly out of Birmingham. You just drive there so someone can tell you why you can't. Still, I did not fret. I had a safety day built in. I'd go tomorrow. I spent the night not in Hawaii but in the suburb of Homewood. I had a plastic cup of Frosted Flakes and went to bed, to dream, I hoped, of Waikiki, Waimea, and poi, which I think is like undercooked cobbler.

I was up at dawn and made it to the airport two hours early, only to hear the gate agents tell me I could not go to Hawaii this day, either, unless I strapped myself to the underside of a frigate bird for the Los Angeles–to–Hawaii leg. Or they could bend me double and put me in a crate with hogs. They did not actually say this, but that was the gist. "Toilet's froze," I heard someone say, when angry travelers demanded an explanation for why the plane could not fly.

I spent the rest of my Hawaiian vacation in the airport Chick-fil-A, till all hope was truly lost. It is what I think of, every time, when I think of Hawaii—ukuleles, and waffle fries.

This Means War

~⌒

WE LIVE BY THE FEUD HERE IN THE SOUTH. We will wait a lifetime to get even with anyone or anything, including an insect, and I believe some insects will wait lifetimes to get even with us. I don't believe this of most things. I don't think there is a caterpillar out there who holds a grudge. But I hate the red wasp, and I am sure the whole species hates me back.

I have heard that in cooler places, preachers spend entire sermons on forgiveness, about how we should love our enemies. Their pulpits are worn smooth with goodwill and polished with human kindness. It sounds like a noble way to be—and I think, sometimes, I could do a little better myself.

Then I step out into the thick air of another Southern summer and am beset by a squadron of hot needles with wings. And I am still a hater, and my heart is a parched and stony place wherein the milk of human kindness soured many swarms ago.

It began in childhood. I owned a beautiful Daisy Red Ryder BB gun with a saddle ring and a leather thong to tie it to my horse—which, in 1968, was a sad, wobbly bicycle. I roamed dirt roads and driveways looking for something to kill.

I drew down on birds and squirrels, but my heart was still soft then, and I couldn't pull the trigger. I searched for things that deserved to die, like water moccasins, brown scorpions, and woolly boogers. The best I could do, usually, was a red wasp. They were too small and erratic in flight to even try to shoot on the wing. So I waited till they lit and drew a careful bead.

I got braver with time and attacked the nest, which resulted in a hateful swarm that was almost human in its nature. They stung me till I retreated inside my grandma's house, where she doctored my wounds with a daub of wet snuff. I quit when I was eleven or so, but the wasps did not relent. I imagined them sitting around telling stories about me, generation after generation.

They stung me walking across the yard. They stung me in the bed. They sting me now.

Some would say it is karma, but being not altogether certain what that means, I respond in my old age with a can of toxic, foaming Bengal Wasp & Hornet Killer. But it's getting harder and harder to run away. I try to shoot them from the air, and sometimes I do. I hoot and do a little dance, which looks sadder the older I get.

Someday, perhaps, I will wander into the yard with an empty can and shoot at wasps that are not actually there. It would be a very Southern thing to do. And I bet one last, mean wasp, the sneaky little devil, will see me down there and jab me one final time, just so he can brag about it.

The Mean Season

⁓⁓

THE *clip-clop* of the mule's ironshod hooves is so slow, the steps so far between, you wonder if it might have died mid-step and is just waiting for a hint of breeze in the hot, wet air to push it on over.

Clip . . .

An eternity . . . *Clop.*

And I am relieved. The atmosphere is already thick enough here in the French Quarter in the misery of late August without throwing a dead mule into the mix. The mule, hauling a pair of parboiled tourists and a guide in a woeful, wilting top hat, creaks and creeps off toward the old St. Louis Cathedral, down a narrow street jammed with perspiring, half-drunk people. The tour guide recites a history of the city as they wobble past, but New Orleans is too old to tell about in one buggy ride, even pulled by a slow-motion mule in a steaming time warp. It takes ages before it finally lurches out of sight. The tall glass in my hand had been filled with ice when I first saw the mule; now it sits in a tepid puddle on the tabletop. I should get up, I think to myself, and do something. So I ask for more ice.

People say this is the worst time of the year to visit, that the place never was intended for August. It takes a whole lot of ice to make it so, but I think New Orleans and summer are like old enemies that have, after hundreds of years, fought to a drunken draw. Having failed to kill it outright, summer tries to smother it a little bit, day by day. I like it here, even in the mean season, the months when eating an oyster can take your life. I'd rather sweat in New Orleans, listening to the iron squeak of an old streetcar, feeling the wind off the wide river on my face, than summer someplace precious.

Before air-conditioning, the rich used to flee, leaving the poor to swelter and perish. Mosquitoes filled the air, and malaria filled the cemeteries. Those days vanished into the cities of the dead, and New Orleans danced and staggered on. But in summer, it seems like you are closer to that deep, dark history, like you can almost feel it on your skin. Take a walk sometime, past the old houses built from steamboat timbers, through the riots of flowers, and see if you don't feel it, too.

This time of year, I don't go to the zoo much, because the creatures are not that active. I doubt the lions would even rouse themselves long enough to eat me, though I did see a nutria give me a hungry look once. I don't drive out to the bayous, for it is hard, in that liquid world, to tell where the earth and water separate, and I find it tough to breathe.

It is better to walk down Royal Street with a Barq's root beer in a cup of crushed ice. It is better to find a fresh mango in the French Market and eat it off the blade of your pocketknife up on the Riverwalk as you watch massive freighters push through the brown water. Then find yourself a cool, dark place to wait out the hottest part of the day—only to realize that you might be there till October.

The Heat Monster

⁓

WHEN I WAS A BOY, when monsters were real, I would see it in the distance, hovering just above the hot, almost liquid blacktop. It had no form, just a thing shimmering, indistinct. Now I know it was the heat itself, distorting the very air. How odd, to see the heat. But when I was small, it was easy to see more in it than that. This was the creature that came in the worst of summer, the boiling eye of it. It was the stunted field, the cracked earth. It was the cloud in a white-hot sky that gave up no rain. Aristotle knew it, and the Romans, and then us, in the American South.

That thing of glimmering heat from my imagination did not have a name, truly, but its season did. We called it the dog days.

The Greeks and Romans believed Sirius, the brightest star in the constellation Canis Major (Greater Dog), ushered in an evil season in late summer, one that boiled seas and soured wine and sent people and livestock into fits. In that season, the Dog Star and our sun hung together in the heavens, one rising, one setting, which, they believed, produced more heat than the planet could stand.

Now, of course, we know it is the tilt of the planet, closer to the sun, that brings the heat, but my grandmother knew better. Ava Bundrum knew there were more things than heaven and earth, and spoke of the dog days the way she would any unnatural thing. She would motion me close, as if the clinging air were listening, wave a cardboard funeral home fan at me like she was giving me some kind of blessing, and tell me to stay out of the pasture, stay out of the woods.

It was more than myth. Dogs went mad, or lay panting, glassy-eyed, and you could not rouse them to play. Food went bad in the dog bowls. Cats, though, did not seem to care. Cats don't ever care.

I can remember children crowded around a rattling box fan, as if it were telling them a story.

I remember strong men going white as chalk, trying to catch their breath.

Bulls went mad and tore through fences. Cows would not give milk, and when they did, it went sour, or tasted of sulfur or onions. Birds flew in the house, a bad omen; it meant someone was going to die. Chickens perished in the coop. Rabies resurfaced, in foxes, usually, and men shot them from the porch.

The gardens withered. You got either quick, violent storms or no rain at all. Mudholes vanished into pieces of hard clay, like someone had smashed a pot on the ground. Frogs perished, which made my grandmother sad; the more frogs, the healthier the land. (Everyone knew that.) Only the insects reveled. Flies and gnats swirled. Mosquitoes danced. And there was nowhere to hide.

Air-conditioning was myth. We put a man on the moon before my family had a window unit. But when we did, when the air blew cool in August, it was like the mean season became myth itself, just another story, like the ones that old people told of the Depression. I guess I am the old people now. I think of the dog days when I see that glimmer on the distant asphalt, but when I get there, it is already gone.

Life in the Slow Lane

YOU NEED TO UNDERSTAND that I love Atlanta. I love sitting over a plate of steamed cabbage and fried chicken at Mary Mac's Tea Room. I love dodging the little old ladies on Cheshire Bridge Road when they peel out of the parking lot at The Colonnade Restaurant after "Ladies Lunch." I love the Falcons, though they break my heart. And I love the Braves, though, as one Atlanta writer liked to say, they "stomped that sucker flat." I even lived here awhile, close enough to the Krispy Kreme bakery to wake up smelling sugar.

What a great city this will be when they finally invent the flying car.

I was on the interstate in Atlanta and moving at the speed of warm lead. No. Wait. . . . I only thought I was moving. It was just a hamburger sack blowing in the other direction. It was a trick of the mind, the way people dying of thirst in the desert imagine an oasis. The sack tumbled on by, and I sighed. Sighing is what you do in Atlanta, when you've exhausted your repertoire of curses and are too forlorn to do any more than rend your hair and gnash your teeth.

To pass the time, I made up songs in my head. (Sung to the tune of "Losing My Religion" by R.E.M.)

> *That's me in the Toyota*
> *That's me in the left lane*
> *Losing my religion*

Or . . .

(Sung to the tune of "Midnight Train to Georgia" by Gladys Knight & the Pips)

> *Oh, I'm not leavin'*
> *In this breakdown lane in Georgia*

But I couldn't think of anything that rhymed with Georgia, so I went back to reading the bumper sticker on the car in front of me for the thousandth time.

HUNKER DOWN, HAIRY DAWGS

Then I thought: What if I die here? What if that is the last thing I ever read in my life?

I lived here for about three years. People ask me if I liked it, and I say that I did. It must be a good town if you're willing to put up with this. Now, for the third year in a row, Atlanta is number one. It's home to the most miserably congested bottleneck in America, the convergence of I-285 and I-85, known as Spaghetti Junction.

The "peak average speed" is 24.7 miles per hour, slower than some tractors. The city is also home to the fourth-worst intersection, the convergence of I-285 and I-75. All in all, seven of the nation's one hundred worst bottlenecks are here, according to the American Transportation Research Institute, which came to those findings by timing trucks.

I don't know if it was purely miles per hour or if blood pressure was also used as a measurement. I think this city has sent more truck drivers to the cardiologist than Little Debbie.

I decided to reward myself. When the HAIRY DAWG in front of

me finally moved again, I headed downtown to The Varsity and got myself two chili dogs with onions, twisted into a little ball of wax paper, an order of onion rings, and a very large Varsity Orange drink. Then I just enjoyed being alive.

I heard some man quoted about how life is about the journey, not the destination. This guy obviously never had to commute from Marietta.

They Must Be Mad

⁓

SOME THINGS we just don't have to think about down here. Cold, frosty things. Which, in my case, is probably a good thing. I like to picture my mind as a bucket, which is filled with all useful things. The more useless things that get dumped into it, the more useful ones spill out over its rim. Some people have plenty of room in their buckets for both, for five gallons of memories, trivia, and even song lyrics. But I have come to realize that mine is very small—not so much a bucket as a teacup.

My point is that here, south of the permafrost, we do not need to contemplate so many things in winter—like, say, a snow shovel, though I guess it would be good for beating fire ants or chiggers to death. We don't have to choose snow tires or mukluks.

That leaves ample room for pineapple upside-down cake and sausage biscuits. I like to think of winter as short—a thing in passing. I like to stand in the drugstore and wonder what SPF would be suitable for a pasty man. I like to think that, any day now, only the early mosquitoes will be biting, not wolverines. My point is, I do not have room in my limited mind for the foibles of chilly men.

So why, for several weeks now, have I been thinking about ice fishing?

It's not the how of it that haunts me. I have read enough about it to comprehend that. It's the why. Why would I drive my pickup onto any one of the Great Lakes, towing a small house behind, which will keep the howling winds from freezing off my lips, nose, and ears? The hut has a heater that (by all logic) should melt a hole in the ice so it swallows us—hut, truck, and all. But this rarely happens, I am told, in part because the ice is so thick and because, even with a heater, it is still cold enough to kill a thin-blooded man.

To even get at the fish, which have somehow not frozen to death, you have to saw out a hole big enough to drop a baited line, a hole that will keep freezing up. I don't know about you, but there is nothing that gets me in the mood for fishing quite like the familiar screaming of a Poulan Pro and the rhythm of an ice ax.

The hole should not be big enough to fall into, drunk, I am told, since I cannot see how anyone could endure this (huddled in the cold and staring down into a tiny hole) if they were sober. But of all things I cannot quite wrap my mind around, this is the most difficult: You have to bring an ice chest out onto the ice to hold your beer. If you just set it outside, it would freeze. I just can't comprehend this.

Maybe the reason it is all stuck in my head is because of the one time I ever witnessed people ice fishing, or at least saw their little plywood huts. I was in Minnesota when I noticed a dark speck, approaching at a lope, on the white ice. As it got closer, I saw that it was a large rodent of some kind, carrying a fish that it had apparently stolen from the camp. In all my time fishing in the sunshine, I never—not even once—had a gopher swim out and steal a speckled trout.

Dear Grumpy Gardener

࿓

D EAR GRUMPY GARDENER, Pestilence Expert, *Southern Living* magazine,

I am really conflicted. I have long loved the blazing intelligence of E. O. Wilson, the biologist, author, naturalist, and myrmecologist (ant dude) who first discovered the fire ant's presence in America. As you know, these bugs originally came to this country on cargo ships at the Port of Mobile in the 1930s but sneaked around awhile before being discovered by Wilson in 1942.

How they went unnoticed for so long still evades me, because being stung by one is like being stabbed with a red-hot knitting needle, and if you get stung by one, you are likely to be stung by the whole congregation. I guess, like most things, we just blamed it on the Devil.

And this is my conflict: Why did Dr. Wilson not get himself a flat-bladed shovel and beat them all to death right then?

I know the higher, nobler reason. E. O. Wilson is the best of us. He loves the littlest creatures and has spent a lifetime in their study, and in so doing, serves and protects not just the ecology of them but of us all. If you hung all his medals around his neck, he would be pinned to the floor. I met him once, at Harvard in 1993. I knew I was in the presence of a great man.

Still, back in 1942, he should have gotten himself a Coke bottle full of gasoline and a Zippo lighter, and sent the tiny SOBs to their ancestors, mound by smoking mound.

I, too, love the littlest things. Ladybugs? Lightning bugs? Even plain ants. I would lie on my stomach, when I was little, and watch them.

The fire ant is something else entirely. If you catch a June bug in your hands, to look at it, it will not call in three thousand of its closest friends to try to sting you to death. The fire ant injects an alkaloid venom that, to me, seems just plain unnecessary, and may bite with its mandibles, just to be mean. It is one of the few things that can hurt you with either end, like an alligator. But it is far worse than an alligator, because you are unlikely to step on an alligator by accident when you take out the trash.

I grew up on farmland in Alabama, working in dirt, beating fire ants off my pants legs. I stepped from swimming holes straight into their mounds and leaped back into the water to drown them, only to see them float away on rafts of their own bodies, probably giggling. I hit their mounds at thirty miles an hour on a riding lawn mower, creating clouds of them; a kind of ant apocalypse settled round me like the wrath of God.

I am not asking you how to kill them, as I know you have strong feelings on this. I know there are baits and other scientific methods, but none give me the joy I derive from a more traditional way. We just knock the top off the mound with a shovel, pour in the gas, set it on fire, and beat them to death as they come out the top. I do not recommend this to suburbanites, as it will likely result in self-immolation. No, all I really need from you is to just tell me: Does this make me a bad person?

Sincerely,
Rick Bragg

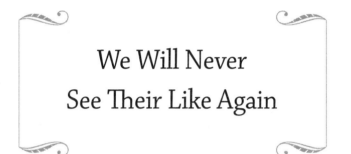

We Will Never
See Their Like Again

The Great Conroy

~

HE LEFT THE MESSAGE every few months, the same message, word for word.

"Bragg? This is Conroy. It is now obvious that it is up to me to keep this dying friendship alive. You do not write. You do not call. But I am willing to carry this burden all by myself. It is a tragedy. Ours could have been a father-son relationship, but you rejected that. And now it is all up to me, to keep this dying (bleep, bleep, bleepity, bleeping) friendship from fading away . . ."

And then there would be a second or so of silence, before:

"I love you, son."

That part always sounded real.

I would always call back, immediately, but the voicemail just told me it was full, always full. I would learn, over decades, that it was full because I was not the only writer or friend he had adopted, or even the only one he left that same message of mock disappointment and feigned regret. But now and then I would actually be there when he called, and we would talk an hour or two about writers and language and why I should love my mother, and he would always, always tell me he had read my latest book, and how he was proud of me.

Then he would tell me how he did not mind that I had neglected our friendship and that his broad shoulders could carry the weight of my indifference, and the phone would go dead.

My God, I will miss that.

Pat Conroy died on the edge of spring. I won't try to add anything to the gilded language said over him; those who have read him know of the elegance there. I just know he was different from others at the top of this craft, different in his generosity. He was a champion, even for those who pretended not to need one.

Some two decades ago, when my first book was just months from publication, he wound up with a bound galley and actually read it all, and sent a message to my publisher with his thoughts. We call such endorsements, inelegantly, "blurbs." This was the best blurb ever written, lustrous and—now that I have had twenty years to consider it—undeserved. But a thousand people since have told me they read it because he told them to, and quote the last line of that blurb to me: "I wept when the book ended . . . and I sent flowers to his mother."

But it was what happened, months later, that mattered most. He and his soon-to-be wife, the fine writer Cassandra King, came to visit my mother in Alabama, and brought her half a German chocolate cake. (My mother was too kind to ask what happened to the other half.) As he left, he offered to take my mother and elderly aunts home with him. "I'll cook for you," he said. He told me later he was impressed by my big brother, and my sister-in-law. He looked in their faces and saw the utter absence of Old South pretension, and fell in love with that, too, a little bit. As he left I knew I was now only the second most popular writer in our home; *The Water Is Wide* is my mother's favorite book. Because of him, we see the good in Santini, and knew that any man, no matter how wounded or damaged, can be a prince of tides. We will miss the words he had still to write.

We will miss a damn sight more than that.

The Talker

⁓

THIS SPRING will be different.

It won't look different in the foothills of the Appalachian Mountains. The black mules will still stand belly deep in the yellow broom sage, sniffing for the new green. Old men will wrestle their tillers across the ground, swatting at the gasoline smoke as they turn their yards into a patchwork of red dirt, buttercups, and wild green onions. Old women will watch the skies for storm clouds and the porch rafters for red wasps.

Still, it will be different, since Uncle Jimbo died. It will be quieter here.

We buried James Bundrum in winter in a beautiful little cemetery in Whites Gap, Alabama, at the foot of those mountains, just west of the Alabama-Georgia line. We buried him at the edge of the old graveyard, in the shade of the woods, beside people he knew, people who shared his last name. But all I could think about was how still it was, and how it was the only time in my life I had ever been in the presence of the man and not heard a grand story, or tale, or lie.

"He was a talker," said my kinfolks, again and again, as they walked away.

He was more than that. In a whole family of great storytellers, he was the greatest. He had the power to tug a person back in time. And in that silence, I could almost hear the times change, and those bridges fall.

In his youth, he had been an MP in World War II and came home to roof a million houses.

He lost two children in a house fire, and his heart broke forever. And though I cannot be sure, I think he buried that agony under his foolishness, beneath that great ability to make anyone smile. It was Jimbo who told me stories of snapping turtles as big as Volkswagens and of catfish that swallowed whole cows. He told me ghost stories that made my knees knock, told tales of run-over dogs that returned to life, and he could talk all day about snakes.

"And, hon," said his daughter, Jeanette, "some of 'em was true."

In his old age, he loafered around, making a circuit from the old Food Outlet grocery to the cemetery to the creek banks and back again. He liked the cemetery. He told me once that it was where a man his age had to go to talk to anybody who could appreciate him.

So it is quiet now. The preacher at the graveside said he knew my uncle was saved, and that his people could take comfort in that. The last time I saw Uncle Jimbo alive, he mentioned he'd stopped lying, and then he told me about going coon hunting with his daddy, back when he was a boy, and stopping to rest on a log that turned out to be a giant snake. Then he told me about a catfish that was so big it clogged a whole creek in Whites Gap. And then he was just gone.

Harper Lee

～⌒

WRITERS, I HEAR, get to be famous in a quiet kind of way. I
have yet to see one on a T-shirt. Their posters appear mostly
in libraries, bookstores, and orderly literary festivals, printed with
good grammar and dignified fonts. People *will* applaud them, with
polite enthusiasm, and might even line up to see them, for a signa-
ture or a handshake, but rarely do they push, hoot, or jostle, even
for the most famous of them. Nelle Harper Lee was too private,
much of her life, even for such as that, and this was part of her
great mystery.

I knew a young writer who wanted to meet her. To him, as with
so many of us who call ourselves that, she stood at the zenith of
what we wanted to be, for she had written a book that mattered,
that had, even in some small way, changed the world. The young
writer just wanted to step onto her porch in Monroeville, and, in a
perfect world, see the lady herself open the door and say . . . well,
anything, "Hello," or "May I help you?" or even "Get off my damn
porch." I cannot recall exactly what happened, but I believe he did
seek her out, and she was polite to him, as I recall.

Me, I was too proud. I waited till I was almost an old man myself,
to go see her. And when I did, I spoke just a few moments about
nothing at all and then left too soon, because I was too polite. I left
with questions unasked and the great mysteries unsolved. I doubt

if she would have told me any of them anyway, if I had been of a pushy mind. But she was kind, and complimentary, and told an Auburn joke, and though it was already clear that macular degeneration and a profound deafness had begun to imprison her, her legendary wit was still there, and that was a fine gift on a spring afternoon, in a small, hot room in a quiet retirement home in Monroeville, Alabama.

It is widely known that people who knew her called her Nelle.

I think I never called her anything but ma'am, and mumbled that. And then, not long after, in February of 2016, she was gone.

But this, in remembering your idols, may not be the worst it could be.

Published in 1960, *To Kill a Mockingbird* was a kind of gospel, north and south, appealing, through the beauty of story, for us to be better than we were, to live up to our finer natures, and not our baser ones, to rise inside our own consciences and not wallow in the mob. I have written that it was not a cure. The meanness depicted in its story endures and, in the modern day, still often triumphs. Yet the hope in it lingers on, and on.

One of the few who did know her, who shared his thoughts with her in writing, was the respected professor, historian, and author Wayne Flynt, who, with his wife, Dartie, corresponded with her across decades, beginning in 1993. In that fine meantime, they wrote of the world as they saw it, of catfish, Mobile eye doctors, Hebrews 13:8, hateful infirmity, C. S. Lewis, Zora Neale Hurston, whether or not Baptists will tell a lie, and if someone told Truman Capote that Kennedy had been shot, he would have claimed to have been driving the car. She asked, in writing, if he would preach her funeral.

He did know her.

"Two things I talked to her about," Dr. Flynt said, "I could never tell while she was alive."

One would seem easy, yet has been debated by scholars for decades: What was the theme of *To Kill a Mockingbird*?

To her, it was simple. It was not just about race, though that will always be the part we most cut ourselves upon, but about all kinds of justice, and fairness, and a sorting out of what it means to get into someone's skin and walk around in it. You never gain any understanding, in a pluralistic society, until you do. She expected smart people, like Flynt, to know this.

In a time "when we needed it as an insight to race, she told it to us in a way that seared our conscience," said Flynt, who is also an ordained Baptist minister. The other question, of why she did not more quickly follow with another book, is still not perfectly clear, even after years of friendship. He believes it is not one answer but many, including the fact that she was never sure she could write another book of such quality.

"Then she looked at me with those sparkling, inquisitive eyes," he said, and told him, more or less, she didn't have to. Then, only at the end of her life, came the sequel, written not after *Mockingbird,* but before.

Flynt put his and his wife's correspondence with Harper Lee into a lovely book called *Mockingbird Songs,* to, finally, "let her voice become part of the conversation," he said.

The best thing about that long friendship was its depth, and that was also its pain. It broke his heart as her deafness and blindness closed in, and confusion followed, to the point she could not always recognize the people she knew that she should know. It is the price you pay, for the joy of it.

Most of us have only what Harper Lee gave us, which was 376 pages, in paperback.

My niece, Meredith, read the book for the first time recently. When I asked what she would remember, she said "the knothole," where Boo Radley left the treasures for the children to find, before it was filled in with cement, to try to kill a friendship that could not be so easily killed.

Everyone has something that stays inside them, from this book. I hear that when Tennyson died, they rang the bells in London all day, longer. Every time I hear a bell, I think of Tennyson.

Every time I hear a mockingbird, I wish I had stayed longer in that hot little room.

Spirit of the Mockingbird

≈

IT IS FOOLISH, I KNOW. But I choose to believe it, how one of these evenings, when the world slows down enough to listen to the falling dusk, we will catch the song of a mockingbird. And maybe we will think about her, and the enduring story she told. Foolishness, sure. Yet how lovely, to think that a person can live forever as long as one last bird sings in the dying light of one more day.

When they told me she had passed peacefully in her sleep in Monroeville, I do not recall a great sadness. Harper Lee passed into legend, into spirit, long ago. I do not claim to have known her; I saw her once, and she was kind and complimentary and I walked away on air. All I truly know, I know through the pages of one great book, and that, as in that birdsong, is where her spirit resides.

Published in 1960, *To Kill a Mockingbird* condemned and attempted to explain the meanness and hypocrisy of her South, while celebrating the fragile notion of kindness and common decency. It was not a cure, and people went on about their meanness unchecked for a long while.

But her story endured, and reminded us, even the sorriest of us, who we could be if only we did not abandon our finer nature.

One of the smartest men I know called it "her gospel," and I am not smart enough to say it any better.

Ms. Lee presented her sermon, as all people of great spirit do, in a remarkable story. My favorite part is the scene she creates in the courthouse as Atticus, failing to save Tom Robinson from a backward jury, exits the silent courtroom, and all the black people in that courtroom, relegated to the balcony, rise in respect. His daughter, Scout, is told to rise, too, to honor her father even in defeat, though it takes her a while to understand. I do not believe much in moral victories, but thick as I am, the beauty and power in that passage still gives me a chill.

Some, apparently stone-blind to the backwardness that would linger as some Southerners substituted racial slurs for legislation to target again the most vulnerable, would question its relevance in a modern world. But Harper Lee's gospel was always there, assigned to high school students by teachers who did their part to spread the great message and open minds. I have heard critics say it was a naïve book, simplistic, but I know a little about our South, how the things that make us most ashamed of our past—and present—are not always our actions but our silence. Her words were our tonic, our balm.

I have written that I did not agree with her in full. Her villains were poor whites, her heroes a frayed gentry, as if poor whites alone had the power to shape the landscape. Her daddy was a lawyer and she told it from her perspective, as was her prerogative as a novelist. But her Atticus, even though too good to be true, would somehow solidify, and take on life. People talk of Atticus as if they sat next to him at Waffle House, or saw him in Target buying Pop-Tarts. That, by God, is a trick.

It remains, in the lore of our people, a sin to kill a mockingbird. But those simple words have taken on a power and beauty and meaning beyond language, to become a thing to live forever.

The Voice of Peace and Power

Billy Graham even made sinners stop and listen

~~~

Written before his death on February 21, 2018

THE WORD coursed through the Southern air when I was a boy. It flew through the pines and across the cotton fields until it was snagged by a raggedy antenna and channeled, hissing and crackling, through the picture tube of a secondhand Zenith TV. We learned of the exodus, of the swallowing of Jonah and the trials of Job, through static and a horizontal roll—until someone went outside and turned the antenna back toward Birmingham. I watched my grandmother press her palms to the warm plastic to be healed, saw kinfolks shake the floorboards in time to the Happy Goodman Family, Dixie Echoes, or Florida Boys, till the preaching resumed from Tulsa, Pensacola, or Baton Rouge. The televangelists and their troubadours would become the soundtrack of our lives, constant, beseeching, and much the same, a kind of white noise for me and my sinful brothers, something to be tolerated till *Gunsmoke* came on.

Only one voice truly transcended, only one got through. Children stopped playing. Old people leaned closer.

"They love their lust, love their sin so much, they don't want God to come . . ."

Only one really reached into that hot little room, and pulled.

"But the day of the Lord will come, like a thief in the night . . ."

I remember thinking, the way a boy thinks, that if I turned the set off, even if I crawled behind the television and jerked the plug out of the wall, that voice, strong and clear and calm, would still be pulling, pulling, and the only way to be free of it was to run out the door and down the road. And then some passing car would probably still bring him into earshot again, its radio tuned to some distant coliseum where a hundred thousand people had come to hear God's Word, through Billy Graham.

"Lust and greed and hate and jealousy . . . the human race stands, at this moment, on the brink . . ."

The face was handsome but fierce, like a lion or an angry hawk, its eyes like drill bits, its jaw set in iron. But mostly it was that voice that got you, that voice that sounded so loud, even in a whisper, it seemed to come at you in color even from a thirty-five-dollar black-and-white. It was never shrill, never strident, never alarmed, even as it told of the end of days. That voice, at least to a little boy, was a voice of peace and power. The other preachers of my childhood had raved and sweated and accused, preached it so hard, as one old man told me, "a feller couldn't live it." And there was some of that in this voice—but only some. It was, in one breath, a doubled-up fist, pounding, driving, at sin, at hypocrites, at the Devil hisself. But in the next breath the voice calmed, welcomed, like a laying on of hands. And sometimes, impossibly, it was all these things, as we think a judge should sound, or a father, or just any good, strong man. Because what the voice mostly did, in all that power, was plead for goodness, and argue against despair.

"And I am ready, for I am a child of God."

My mother never missed him. Many nights, after taking in other people's laundry or flipping hamburgers at a truck stop cafe, she listened to that voice, heard the calm insistence that this hard life was not all there was, and she was soothed. It was a Southern voice, but proper, educated-like, but not too proper, not the voice of a man who would look down on her even if he stood somewhere very high. More than anything, the voice seemed like a great river, deep and warm and too strong to swim against.

"Me and your Aunt Juanita went to this tent revival once on the Roy Webb Road, to hear this little preacher," she said. "His voice was angry—he was mad when we got there. And I told your Aunt Juanita to get her big pocketbook and let's go home. Some preachers preach from an angry spirit—they can't hide it in their voice. Billy Graham never preached from anger. It ain't the one who shouts the loudest that you remember what they said. And even when he got old, his voice didn't change." She believes there is God's hand in that, and she is my mother so that must be true.

The calm people heard in Graham's voice was a simple manifestation of faith, said Chris Roberts, a journalism professor at the University of Alabama, and a lifelong Baptist. It was the voice of a man, Roberts said, "who knew how the scoreboard was gonna read at the end . . . and it wasn't too late to change jerseys."

"The most prominent place in hell is reserved for those who are neutral on the great issues of life. . . . We will stand as a nation to give account of our stewardship here."

Millions were saved through his ministry. Only Christ saves, he explained, but there is no denying his voice called them—some used the word "seduced"—a stadium-full at a time. Before satellites and worldwide ministries—he was a pioneer and master of mass media—he ushered them down the aisles of churches and tent revivals. The late columnist and author Lewis Grizzard once wrote that Graham sounded—and looked—as he imagined God. Some were offended. Lightning never struck Lewis that I know of. But millions knew Graham was God's messenger, knew the voice of a dairy farmer's son from Charlotte was bouncing not from a satellite but someplace higher. In 1959, a woman in Australia said that, in the midst of thousands, she heard him speak to her alone. In that same voice, he counseled presidents, Republican and Democrat, and won the respect of even nonbelievers, preaching inclusiveness instead of division: Dogma would not open the gates of heaven; one must accept Christ and live a good life. That meant salvation, and improved this world for us all. Maybe that is what a prophet is. I only know of that voice I heard as a boy, and the warmth and warning that traveled with it on the air.

"Believers look up, take courage. The angels are nearer than you think."

The Best of Who We Are

⁓

I DID NOT CROSS THE THRESHOLD of many churches when I was a boy, I guess because I was afraid the aisle would crack wide open and flames would shoot into the air. We mostly went for the Christmas play and for dinner on the ground. Still, I like to remember it, remember black suits over white socks and grandmothers with their arms full of fat babies and their giant purses stuffed with butterscotch candies and Juicy Fruit. I remember how pretty the hymns were, even if Sister So-and-So couldn't carry a tune in a wheelbarrow, bless her heart. I remember how the old people raised their hands as they sang "I Saw the Light." I figured they were waving at angels only they could see. I even remember the sermons, how men in clip-on ties stood before their congregations on a low dais, to show they did not think they were somehow better than us. I can still see them raise tattered Bibles to the rafters and preach on human kindness and peace.

This was the 1960s in an all-white church in Alabama, and in the turmoil of that time, those men of God could have preached politics, could have used their modest pulpits to stroke the resentments of the place and time like a mean cat. But they chose to do otherwise. They did not give in to expediency, to opportunism. They preached, instead, about loving your brother and your sister.

They asked us to be generous if we could, to help the sick and the poor. They also preached on hell, of course.

It may be that it didn't take, in the long run. But it was perhaps the first time I understood the power of words and formed a belief in my people, which I have retreated into when I was hurt to my bones by the rhetoric of this new New South. I guess nostalgia is our sanctuary in sorry times.

Like many people, I watched in sadness and disgust as the images from Charlottesville, Virginia, flickered across my television, watched a man steer his car into a crowd of counterdemonstrators, killing a young woman and wounding many others. I am told these white supremacists believe they are justified in their actions, by the rhetoric of demagogues old and new, and are encouraged by their modern-day leaders who don't hide in the dark woods but live in the political spotlight.

I don't write much about politics or news. But I recognize evil when I see it, and stupidity, and banality. I hear that many of the people who marched in Charlottesville were Southern men, but I didn't know them. I saw men in custom-molded neo-Nazi helmets and designer flak jackets and hundred-dollar aviator glasses. It used to be that all they needed to dress up to hate was a good white sale. Southerners should be angry to be dragged down among them, by even the vaguest association. We can say that's not happening, but it is.

I did not grow up gentle, or much enlightened. I grew up in an everyday racism; the Confederate flag license plates that rode on the front bumpers of our pickups hurt others like a thumb in the eye. It took me a while to get it, but it came to me, even as a boy. I do not need a statue or flag to know that I am Southern. I can taste it in the food, feel it in my heart, and hear it in the language of my kin. It may be that I only remember this through the eyes of a boy, but I believe I heard the best of who we are in those sermons in that little bitty church.

The Dancing Skinny

IT RAINED EVERY DAY for three months, from late fall till spring. I'm sure a weak sun came out once or twice but never long enough to get used to. Mostly it was dank and cold, and the sky was low, like the ceiling of a coal mine, the clouds the color of asphalt. By March the low places ran with muddy water and washed whole lifetimes away, and storms tore up some parts of the South like they were held together with shoeboxes and glue. Things rusted that never had, doors swelled and jammed, and roots of hundred-year-old trees lost their grip in the liquid soil and fell under their own weight. It even caused a kind of moldering in the mind, an absence of optimism, like we had tracked the red mud into our finer nature. I have often heard old people in Alabama pray for rain, but never so hard against it. My mother began to see it as a sign, and it did seem odd, as the weeks slogged by. The weatherman offered no hope, night after night; he might as well have been a cardboard cutout with a fixed, final forecast, and the rains fell, till the end of the world.

Or it might be it all just seemed that way, on the day a good dog died.

The people who discarded her, who threw her away, called her something else, but we never knew that name. We called her Skinny, because she was two dogs high and half a dog wide. She was so lean, so long-legged and light, she seemed to glide without effort or even the pull of gravity when she flashed through the pines and the rocky places up high, running down a deer or just some distant sound, and she would sprint across a mountain to make sure a scent on the breeze presented no threat to her people, her porch, her place. She was just a stray that walked up one day in the yard, part redbone, foxhound, and a dozen other bloods, an old-fashioned, outside, Alabama brown dog that survived abandonment and starvation and bloody battles with coons and coyotes and wild dogs. We fed her and so she became part of the place, for seven years or more, till the hateful combination of a rare tick-borne disease and pneumonia—I blamed the constant cold and damp for that—finally killed her, early on a Sunday afternoon.

We never knew her age, either, but believe she was about eight or so when she died, with us long enough to get used to, to root out a place in our minds. I have never prayed a lot and, frankly, as a prolific, almost redundant sinner, have seldom asked for or expected help from on high. But as the nice, sad lady at the vet's office handed her to me, covered in a Winnie the Pooh blanket, topped with her empty collar, I cynically wondered, *Well, Lord, do you reckon you could stop the rain long enough to let us get her in the ground?*

But I guess you don't stand much of a chance with the Creator when you ask for something as a smart aleck, and it rained all day, again. My brother Sam and I took a mattock and two shovels into a corner of the pasture and hacked through the vines and privet bushes to a dormant orchard of old peach, apple, and plum trees. There, next to a beautiful German shepherd we called Pretty Girl and a goat with no name, we mucked out her grave. It seemed a miserable place, in the gloom, but not if you had seen Skinny before, in the sunshine. She had gone into the vines and thorns of the tangled orchard after big rabbits every day of her new life. She treed a million squirrels and kept one poor possum hostage in a wild plum tree for what seemed like the better part of a year. She was a hound, and so believed it was her prerogative to hunt and hunt *everything,* even tracking the flight of a timber wasp or a falling leaf, and the fact that she did not differentiate a raccoon from the FedEx man should not be held against her, in the story of her life. My point is, she was something special in motion, running that mountain, and maybe this old pet cemetery was not such a bad place for a dog to lie, here in a tangle where the fat rabbits thumped around over your bones.

Even in the muck it had been hard-digging, because of the roots, and, being old men, we took a while to get straightened up good when we were through. We looked at each other when we did, a little confused about what to do next. It seemed like something needed to be said over her, but there was enough of the lingering Pentecostal left in us to prevent it. The foot washers don't pray for dogs, for there is no soul in them, or so we had always been told. Dogs are creatures of this world alone, and this was the end of her. So we just stood, leaning on our shovels as we had when we were boys, and let the rain soak us to the bone.

"Well," said my brother, finally, "she was a good dog."

We could, both of us, risk that much hell. We slid the tools into the back of the pickup and rode through the waterlogged pasture half expecting to mire up to the axle, and as we inched through the spongy grass, I thought about how it was that almost all dog stories are the same, how they begin and end the same, a trajectory as sure as death, as sorrow. And then you move on, to a new arc, a new story, and another short life. Our place, in the Appalachian foothills, had always been a magnet for strays, for discarded dogs, so we usually got them for only part of their lives, and an even shorter arc. But this death, this story, was different somehow, and struck me harder, as if her place in the longer journey, the arc of the people she watched over with almost human, intelligent eyes, would not so easily fade.

That would come to be, as the months tumbled by. At first there was only this empty place in the landscape, a bleak quiet and a stillness so disproportionate for such a small animal, a thing so bad you knew it just had to give, because no one grieved for a dog like this. And the funny thing was, she wasn't even my dog.

I don't know who threw her away, but he was a son of a bitch, whoever he was. She had been a living skeleton when she came over the ridgeline and just sat there, patient, starving, watching the house below and the people who came and went. It was clear she had doffed a litter of pups in the past few weeks, somewhere, but though we searched we could not find them; from the look of her, they must have perished in the woods, but I guess we'll never know that, either. She came down only when we called. My mother made her a skillet of water gravy and fed her half a pone of cold cornbread, and she became a part of us, or maybe it is more accurate to say she took possession of the place, of the pastures, the mountain, and the humans on it. It would be foolish to say she belonged to us. Skinny did not belong to anyone, really.

She tolerated and looked over the livestock, which she seemed to regard as dumb beasts fit only for keeping the grass gnawed down, and sometimes she seemed to look at two-legged beings in the same way. Strange humans were to be distrusted and chased away with strong bluffs and barks, because she never bit a soul. But it was clear, quickly, that we were hers, and she asked for and received just enough petting from her humans to remind her that she was *the* dog, and then she would turn away and go do something important.

From the first week, she began to protect us, haranguing the meterman, distant kinfolks, a suspicious chipmunk, the hopelessly lost Papa John's driver, and the occasional wandering Jehovah's Witness. Her philosophy seemed to be: Growl at 'em all, chase 'em all a quarter mile at least, and let God sort 'em out. And sometimes, purely by the law of averages, she found a proper villain this way.

Before Skinny arrived, a gray fox, well fed and as big as a Labrador, had killed every living thing on the mountain it could catch. It killed every chicken my mother had, and her ducks and ducklings, and even ran down a cat every now and then. Then it would sit halfway up the ridgeline, so close my mother could see it through her back windows, and sing to her, mocking. It was such an eerily human, menacing thing that my mother named it: Henry. She had never met a Henry she could bear, and this one was no different. It may sound like hyperbole, if you are not an old woman in a dark house cut into a mountainside.

Skinny, as soon as she could stand without trembling, put Henry on the run, and when he came back, she did it again, and again, and again. She never caught Henry, not that we are sure of, but she harassed him so long and so completely that he abandoned his honey hole on Mark Green Road and vanished into memory. My mother thinks she can hear him even now, singing, but so very faint, as if he knows where the property line is, and remembers, somehow, that a skinny dog used to roam here, and might still.

Skinny stalked the coyotes, a new menace that had just appeared, like wraiths, in the pasture with my mother's tiny Sicilian donkeys. She burst into their midst, snapping and howling, fearless, and scattered them. They left this place as if they had never been, though, and in the spirit of Henry, sometimes we heard them in the far distance, wailing. Skinny did the same with the wild dogs that roamed through here, but they were slower to run, and she earned some scars, including a thin, black line against her fine face.

Skinny never, ever came in the house, and slept up high, on the seat of the old Yanmar tractor, where she could look down upon the land and the livestock that were in her charge. But now and then, on a cold night, she would travel to the far end of the property, where she had learned to open the front door of my little brother's house. She would come in, invited or not, and crawl up on the foot of the bed, and sleep till about an hour before dawn, then come back across the ridgeline for biscuits at my mother's house. "I called her January," said my little brother, Mark, because she only appeared to him in the cold.

But for a long time, there seemed no joy in her; she seldom played much, for a young dog, and if you threw a stick or a ball, she would just look at you, as if you were numb between the ears. It took years for that to change, but it did. She would follow the familiar cars and trucks up the drive, and when you opened the door, she would place both paws on the running board and peer inside, until you spoke to her or petted her. Of course, it being Skinny, it might have been just another kind of surveillance, a trick she was playing on us, to make sure we were not trying to sneak something past her, into her yard, onto her mountain.

Finally, in the last two years of her life, she started acting like a dog. The thing I remember most is the odd way she would greet me, whenever I—or anyone she recognized—stepped from the car. She would go suddenly and completely silly, and would hop across the driveway, one paw stuck straight out as if she were pointing, and sometimes she would dance on her back legs, if only for a second or two, then go back to being her serious and intelligent self. But it was too late. I caught her dancing, caught her being glad to be alive.

She did not seem to mind being the only dog on the place. But people are a low species, compared with dogs, and so were certain to clutter up her perfect isolation sooner or later.

First, it was Puppy who came, a small mixed-breed feist, beagle, and Lord knows. He had lived the first two years of his life utterly ignored inside a chain-link fence, fed and watered but never petted or even spoken to. Puppy appeared in the yard as a kind of canine basket case, scared of everything, and when I tried to pick him up and put a collar on him, he tried to eat my face. I was afraid Skinny would not tolerate him, would run him off, but I swear she seemed to understand that he was a damaged creature, and so chose to ignore him, and even let him trail behind her, at a distance, when she ran the land. I have always been suspicious of people who tried to imbue some kind of magic on their dogs, and I am saying this is so, here. I just think her instincts were both fierce and kind, and if that is not a good dog, I don't know what one looks like. Puppy seemed destined for a life of woe, without even a real name, but after he found a home here—and Skinny's acceptance—I tried again to put a collar on him, and he tried again to eat my face. I named him McGraw, after the cartoon character Quick Draw McGraw, and had it stamped on his collar, which, five years later, still hangs from a nail in the garage.

Then, it was Speck, my dog. He had been the alpha in a pack of wild dogs, till he was replaced, violently, and run off to starve. I fed him after I saw him waiting, watching from the ridge, a beautiful long-haired dog that was part Australian shepherd, red heeler, and blue heeler, with a striking spotted face, but discarded, I believe, because he was blind in one eye. He ate, warily, then, fortified, ran away to fight his way back into the pack. They tore him up badly this time.

The next day I found him on the driveway in a puddle of blood, and he let me pick him up and take him to the vet, who glued and stitched him back together, though it took a while for his left ear to lay right against his head. He, like Skinny, believed he was responsible for patrolling the land, but he, unlike Skinny, seemed dumb as a damn turnip, and mostly spent his days harassing the thousand-pound mule, which could have kicked him to death at any second. But he was glued to me, when he was not antagonizing the equines or trying to herd my eighty-two-year-old mother across the yard. We named him Speck, after the girlfriend of a long-ago distant cousin. The young woman had so many freckles that my grandfather named her the Speckled Beauty, and there are worse ways to name a dog, I suppose. Unlike Skinny, Speck, once he had rediscovered people, needed people, needed them badly. In some ways, in a time when my own health failed for a bit, I needed a dog of my own, but that, as we used to like to say in this business, is another story.

Skinny responded to Speck with growls, and whipped him, three or four times, across the yard. She would look at me accusingly as if to say, *I will never forgive you for bringing this stupid creature into my realm,* but mostly she ignored him. Sometimes I would catch her just watching him, especially when he was barking furiously in the face of the mule, in the same way, as children, we used to watch reruns of *The Three Stooges.*

Now and then, she let them both run with her, almost as if she were teaching them, and they would all flash through those trees, Skinny determined, the others stupidly joyful, and it was such a beautiful thing. And my mother would see me watching, because little happens here that that old woman, even mostly blind now, does not see.

"What you lookin' at?" she asked.

"Just the dogs," I said.

Just the Dancing Skinny, and the Speckled Beauty, and the Puppy McGraw.

I guess the other dogs missed her, when she was gone. The truth is, I am not sure either one of them was smart enough to miss anything except maybe supper. They, too, challenged every car that came up the drive, though McGraw was a timid and trembling boy who tried to keep a half acre between him and any threat, and Speck could not see well enough, on one side, to make out much of anything. He was fearless, though, as Skinny had been, if a little suicidal. He still accosted the massive mule, which just regarded him with a kind of bewilderment. He wanted to herd it, and it did not want to be herded, but I guess he forgot that every night when he went to sleep, and went down the hill to the pasture every single day, expecting a different result. A head doctor in Birmingham told me that is what mental illness is, but I do not know if it applies to dogs. My point is, you just naturally miss a smart dog, and the things they do.

In time my grief did give, not because I forgot Skinny or replaced her, but because I found that it was not so hurtful, in time, to remember. I would see the goofy Speck running wide open between the trees, and, I swear, I could see that skinny brown dog running ahead. It is still awful, that absence, but it is easier to recall the times before, and now and then my brothers and I will even say, "Hey, you remember when ol' Skinny . . . ," and sometimes the memory makes you sick at heart and sometimes it just resurrects a good dog, for a little while. I don't know if dogs go to heaven or not; a human lifetime, the arc of it, may be the closest to eternity that dogs will come, at least as long as you remember them.

The thing that haunts me is my second-to-last visit to the vet, when the people there tried to save her life, and I went to see her. She came out of her crate and stood as I petted her, and then, being a smart dog, just turned and went back into her cage without being told, as if she gave up, as if she knew. That is foolish, of course. No dogs are that smart, are they?

I know, if the arc of my life continues for any time at all, I don't want a smart dog again.

But then, she wasn't my dog.

Return of the Goat Man

━⁙

SPRING HAS ALWAYS BEEN AMBIGUOUS down here, a vague thing, maybe because winter is so ill-defined. Mount Cheaha does not have an ice cap. One does not skate the Tombigbee River.

Winter can be 12 degrees on a Tuesday, and thick with mosquitoes and humidity by Thursday afternoon. Where I am from, you know spring has arrived when you see old men respooling line on their Zebco 202 fishing reels, and the buttercups push up from their beds in old tires half buried in the red dirt and winter rye. Once, when I was a boy, it meant it was time for the Goat Man to arrive, but I have not been a boy for some time.

Some people, people unaccustomed to the long, rolling nothing of a cotton field, would have said there was not much to do in Spring Garden, Alabama, in 1965. We fought the boredom, my big brother and I, the best we could. We rigged a trapeze in the barn; that ended in blood. We waited long hours at the highway, till truck drivers threw us sticks of Juicy Fruit. And we went to see the Goat Man.

He did not arrive in our little community in a car, but in the most raggedy conveyance I had ever seen, a clanking, clattering wagon pulled by a dozen big goats, with a dozen more—some tethered, some on the honor system—trailing behind. The man himself walked alongside, usually with a baby goat, often an orphan, cradled in his arms. He looked a little like Santa Claus, if Santa had dressed himself from a north Georgia flea market, and smelled of woodsmoke and goat. His long, gray-white beard hung on his ravaged face like Spanish moss on an ancient, lightning-blasted tree, and the elbows of his longhandles poked through big holes in his shirt. He was an old man, then; he'd been a wanderer most of his life.

"Your daddy took y'all to see him, and my daddy took us to see him," my mother told me. His real name was Ches McCartney, and he had a home, before the Great Depression took his Iowa farm and set him to walking. He would clank and clatter across the roads of the country for four decades, freezing, broiling, but always moving, eventually settling across the state line in Georgia. In time, wrote author Jerome Chandler, he became a folk hero, and children lined the roads when word spread, house to house, that the Goat Man was comin' to their town.

In Spring Garden, a tiny place with one country store, cars pulled to the side of the road, creating the only traffic jam in its history. He made camp there that night, and we lined up four deep to watch him slice an apple and feed it to a baby goat.

"What does he do?" I asked my daddy.

"He don't do nothin'," Daddy answered, and I was very small then but I think there was some envy in him, for that.

Great Southern artist Larry Martin did a lovely picture of him. It hangs in my hall, a simple black-and-white drawing, one of my favorite things. I heard the Goat Man died, and I hate that.

Now we just have the calendar to go by.

The Picture Taker

THE PEOPLE WHO RAN NEWSPAPERS and galleries and contests called him an artist and even a genius, a self-taught wizard who could point his lens at a thing and steal a sliver of it, of what made it beautiful or special or just heartbreaking. He could shoot an old woman on a porch and make you feel every pain she ever lived through, and carry you to the lip of every grave she ever dug. He could shoot a boy balancing on a rail and make you feel the possibility of the track—and life—that stretched out before him. He made Clay County look like the most beautiful place on earth. He was almost too good at his craft, because he could make poverty and suffering beautiful, for a snap in time. He could even make you see color, in black and white. That is why the people who run newspapers and galleries and contests honored him, and spoke of him in noble tones, and called him all those forty-dollar things.

The people he shot, though, did not even call him a photographer.

To them, he was just the picture taker.

I think, now, that they honored him as much as anyone ever has.

I worked with Ken Elkins for years when I was a young man

and he was whatever age he chose to be at the time. I figured out, after a while, that I was receiving a gift, with every mile we drove in whatever raggedy, falling-apart contraption Ken was piloting at the time.

It was not what he said; he might have looked like Mark Twain but he did not talk like him. It was how he moved around people, how easy and gentle and peaceful, so that people who had plenty of reason to distrust men in khaki pants and clip-on ties would suddenly go at ease, and tell their stories.

He was not taking, as most journalists do. He was just borrowing, and they could tell that, and one day, when he happened by a place again, he would drop off a picture, to show the people what he had seen in the creases in their face, or in their clouded eyes.

People where I am from, people Ken made a career photographing, know when they are being used. Some of them never forgave James Agee and Walker Evans, for *Let Us Now Praise Famous Men*. But there was never anything to forgive, with Ken.

My friend Chris Roberts, who worked with Ken, too, said it better than I can: "When you drove down Alabama 21 and never hung a right on all those dirt roads you always wondered about, you felt better knowing that Ken had been there and had seen it better than you ever would."

I remember, a long, long time ago, when he and I were ordered to do a story on the man who dug Paul "Bear" Bryant's grave. It was a fine idea as far as an editor's ideas go, but Ken's truck broke down in Irondale.

But the best time was the last time, on a trip into Clay County. I was leaving soon for the *St. Petersburg Times,* and Ken and I drove along a ridgeline that fell away to a beautiful valley, the sunlight strong and clear and the land below a patchwork of green fields and deep green pines and red dirt.

He did not talk in poetry, like I said.
But he kind of did, then.
"Ain't nothin' in Florida, son, like that."
"I guess not," I said.
"Ain't nothin', no where," he said, "like that."

Faux Southern

Keeping It Real

ぐ

I SAW A TAG on the back of a big SUV that proudly proclaimed its driver to be SUTHUN.

I think this would be a good thing for some of my kinfolks, the ones who are still drinking, in case they wake up one morning after a twelve-pack, having forgotten in which region they went to bed. I understand the need to stamp it into metal. It can be confusing these days.

I saw about ten thousand people at the grocery store searching for yogurt, passing up a perfectly good rack of pork rinds. I saw sleds for sale in the window of a hardware store, in Birmingham.

Hardly anyone makes cornbread anymore, even from a mix. And they wear John Deere hats just to appear ironic.

I saw a great sign (painted on a skyscraper) advertising professional hockey in Tampa. It must take a lot of Frigidaires to make an icy spot that wide in the Florida heat.

My point is that the South has changed so much that some people feel they will just float away, perhaps to New Jersey, and some try to anchor themselves with clichés, clutching at magnolias. My people never had much luck with magnolias.

Our South grows from a stone garden, the cemetery where we have buried the treasure—the answer to what Southern is. Some of the names have worn away but not their language. It sings up from the ground.

My Uncle John's daddy, Homer Couch, is here. He wore overalls every day of his life and used to scare us by taking out his teeth. He raised tall cotton and wide hogs and married a woman named Mag. He liked to say, of shiftless men: "He ain't lazy. He was just born tired." When he died, the South shrank a little.

Jimmy Sweat is here. He married my Aunt Sue, drove hot rods, and had the shiniest penny loafers I ever saw. Near the end of his life, his daughter Connie would take him to get fish in a box, though sometimes he seemed unaware. On one trip, he looked over at her and said, "Connie Sue, I just love your guts." He wasn't saying he loved her toughness, her devotion. He was saying he even loved her guts.

Jim Bennett would have understood. He drove a dump truck for my Uncle Ed, though not very well. He drove it right into a house but wasn't fired. My Uncle Ed knew what a man's livelihood meant. "I love that man," Bennett once said of him. "I even love his guts, and the ol' belly that carries 'em."

My Grandma Ava is here, though it is still hard to believe—Ava, who balled up her fist and shoved it under the nose of her husband, after he'd had a few. "I'll knock you out and no water hot!" she told him. I do not even know what that means, but it still beats the heck out of a cliché.

When I forget who I am, I will wander in the weeds among them all, till I find my way again.

There's a Tear in My Beer

⁓

PEOPLE TELL ME I AM TOO NEGATIVE, that the modern world fits me like a thrift-store suit. I tell them to shut up. I do not know when, precisely, I turned the corner from hopeful open-mindedness and slammed headfirst into that dead end where curmudgeons go to die. But I am pretty sure I was trying to find a decent country music station when it happened.

I blame modern country music for all my miseries. I do not blame George Jones, who really did go to the liquor store on a riding lawn mower when they took away his car keys. I do not blame Patsy Cline, who was touched by God, and certainly not Hank Williams, who may have been touched by something different but sang the pain of my people so beautifully that they could bear this life for one more day.

I do not blame Waylon Jennings or Johnny Cash or Freddy Fender, who promised, his voice aquiver, to be there before the next teardrop falls. I do not blame Merle Haggard, "Mexicali Rose," the Wichita lineman, or the year that Clayton Delaney died.

I do not, at least not very much, blame the day mama socked it to the Harper Valley PTA, or Porter Wagoner, who had more unnecessary stuff on his suit than a Shriner's hat. And I certainly do not blame the boys from Fort Payne, the group Alabama, who sang the Southern story.

Papa got a job with the TVA
He bought a washing machine and then a Chevrolet

You don't hear much poetry emanate from the speakers of a 1974 Firebird, but the first time I heard that song, I knew they were singing about us, for us. It used to be, when you were down, you could just turn on country radio and listen to your history, sung by people who seemed to know heartache as an old friend, who sounded like they had once slung a wrench, or fist-fought another man through a fog of Winstons, or owed their soul to the company store.

New country is as country as a black turtleneck, all hat and no cow. It is bland, but more than anything it is a formula of clichés, stitched together by pretty people who have never, it seems, picked a row of okra or packed for Panama City in a paper bag from Piggly Wiggly. They sing in exaggerated accents about tractors, but you know they never had to go looking for their class ring in the roadside weeds after their girlfriend flung it there.

The young people, of course, love them; they think George Strait is a land bridge between Russia and Alaska.

A friend told me they aren't posers, these newer stars; they're what America is. I told him to shut up.

Then I spun my radio dial, searching for a steel guitar, or the words *Take the ribbon from your hair.*

I swear, if I was trapped for long in a vehicle with modern country on the radio, I would fling myself from the speeding car.

I guess it is age. I am sure my ancestors, who cried when Marty Robbins sang about bullet-riddled cowboys south of the border, thought Willie Nelson badly needed a barber, and Jesus.

Out in the West Texas town of Laredo
I fell in love with a Mexican girl

Hot Chicken Is So Not Cool

⁓

THE SIGN on the side of the food truck read: HOT CHICKEN.
"Do you like it hot?" inquired the nice lady inside.

She was a hundred, and in a hairnet. I do not believe she was flirting with me.

"Yes, please," I said, and then I winked at her, in case I had misread the situation. I did not want her to think I was stuck up.

I was in Nashville, and everyone I saw told me that hot chicken was the thing to eat. It was hip, it was cool, and it was happening; indeed, the hippest and the coolest were said to frequent "hot chicken joints," which sounded like something you might stagger into on a back alley in Bangkok, with a gang of drunken Finnish sailors.

So I demurred. I had decided that such a restaurant was too cool for me, like tattoo parlors, and hookah joints, and the Banana Republic. It seemed like the kind of thing that could lead to questionable behavior. One day you order some hot chicken; the next morning you wake up with your belly button pierced and a picture of David Hasselhoff tattooed on your posterior. Point me to a prayer meetin'.

Then, like some dark magic, the hot chicken came to me, rolled right up to me as I walked down the street, like it was fate. Now I know the truth of it: Hot chicken is the fowl of the Devil. He drives a panel truck in Nashville with a sizzling, popping, deep-fat fryer, and his minion looks a lot like Aunt Bee.

For those who have never been exposed, you should understand that this is not spicy chicken, highly seasoned, or even hot by any reasonable standard. I like my chicken to have a kiss of cayenne; I do not mind if it makes me sweat, or even leaves a little burn on my lips.

Nashville hot chicken—at least the bird I had—is not that. It was too hot to consume as food, too hot to stand, and tasted as if it had been marinated in ghost pepper and kerosene. It made my eyes water and my nose run, causing me to rub both of them with my contaminated hands. I went blind. My nose was seared from the inside. I wept and staggered in circles, right in front of the War Memorial. I spiked the offending chicken into a trash can, and wondered, seriously, if I needed medical attention, but could not bring myself to admit to a nurse that I had injured myself with a three-piece dinner.

I cracked the seal on a soft drink and poured it down my throat, but the Devil's chicken could not be extinguished. It had to be flushed from the eyes and nose, like paint thinner, or nuclear contamination.

I am a live-and-let-live man, but it seems to me that some people will do anything to be hip, even immolate themselves from the inside. I blame reality television, where Yankee food-show hosts are fed combustible crawfish and tongue-numbing gumbo, for effect. Good food is not like that. In good food, you taste food, taste seasoning, not an overpowering heat. Everything else is sideshow.

I cannot, of course, condemn all hot chicken. But I'll never look at a panel truck—or a chicken—the same way again.

The Chariots of My People

THE TRUCK BLOCKED OUT a good part of the world around it, kind of like an eclipse, but with TOYOTA stamped on its behind. A new, hulking four-wheel drive with a bolt-on toolbox, big mud tires, and a lift kit that jacked its floorboard up to my eyebrows, it rumbled into the lot and elbowed its way into a parking space. It idled there a second or two longer than seemed necessary, growling and snorting like the big dog it was, and when the driver turned off the switch, you could at least hear the world again, though still in shade. The door opened, and I expected to see a Wolverine boot, or a Timberland, or anything with a steel toe swing out.

Instead, a pointy high heel clicked onto the asphalt.

Now how, I wondered for a full, dull-witted second, did that man get his foot into that little bitty shoe? My Aunt Juanita drove trucks, and my Aunt Jo, and Aunt Edna, just not in a stiletto.

Of all the changes in my South, perhaps the hardest to fit inside my head is the metamorphosis of the pickup truck. I grew up in trucks; I feel good in them. They are the chariots of my people.

There are those down here who say if they can't get to heaven in a Chevy, they'd just as soon stay home.

It's not that I was surprised to see a woman in a big truck; my

Aunt Juanita drove a silver-and-blue Silverado till she was eighty-two. It was the shiny nature of the truck, and the shoe, that just didn't seem right.

It used to be, when you saw a truck, it meant work, and not just any kind of work. Look in the back and there would be six feet of logging chain going to rust, a half bottle of brake fluid, and a shovel and mattock. Some people also rode around with a few crushed empty cans of PBR, but that was because they did not love the Lord.

"Ain't you afraid somebody'll steal that mattock?" I once asked my Uncle Ed.

"Won't nobody steal nothin' to work with," he told me.

I asked him why, then, he kept his chain saw locked in the cab, and he told me to be quiet.

Trucks, at that time, came in mostly two varieties, and most people stood by their brand, till the grave. A quarter century ago, I moved from Los Angeles to New York, and was told a full-size 1986 Ford Bronco would be hard to park in the Theater District. So I offered it, for free, to my brother Sam.

He said he believed he'd just as soon not.

"It's free. You can have it. It's a good truck," I said.

"It's a Ford," he said.

"It's a free Ford," I said.

He just shook his head. He was a Chevrolet man. He pronounces it "Chiv-a-Lay," the way it is supposed to be, and we, traditionally, are the kind of people who have bumper stickers that claim I'D RATHER PUSH A CHEVY THAN DRIVE A FORD. Ford people have one that goes the other way around, kind of like Alabama-Auburn jokes. "You ort to 'a' knowed better," he told me.

Some people, of course, drove a Dodge. We will not speak about this.

But it used to mean something, to drive a truck. If you did, you knew how to sling a wrench, or lay a brick. You hauled manure in it, or at least sand. You owned a hydraulic jack, and a four-way lug wrench.

I have a good friend who drives a truck. He is an insurance man. He ought to be ashamed of himself.

Nissan makes a big ol' truck. They call it, no foolin', a Titan. But I ain't never seen a shovel in back of one.

The Abominable Biscuit

I AM A CROTCHETY RELIC. If you ask me how I am doing, I will respond, "Fine . . . but it's early."

It may not be my fault, completely. Part of it is age. I used to go in the drugstore and buy a Hershey's bar and a yo-yo. Now I go in the drugstore and buy drugs. You are unlikely to skip down the sidewalk clutching a three-month supply of metformin and a quart bottle of amlodipine. And reading glasses. I am always losing my reading glasses.

The rest of it we will blame on the hotel breakfast buffet, the nightmarish twenty-first-century phenomenon dishonestly referred to as a "hot bar." I think that is where I turned the corner from optimist and went stumbling off down the path to miserable old geezer. I believe, somewhere between the desiccated bacon and scrambled eggs so awful there is no known word, I just lost hope.

Maybe it would be easier if I were not a Southerner, who grew up on breakfasts that made waking up a joy. There were soft scrambled eggs with crumbled sausage, thick slab bacon, soft biscuits, milk gravy, sliced tomatoes, fresh cantaloupe. My mother, my aunts, even my uncles made it an art. In lean times, they turned fried bologna and biscuits with water gravy into a delicacy.

But that is a million miles from the canned heat of an expense-account hotel.

I travel a bit. My people, who have no interest in leaving northern Calhoun County unless it slides into a sinkhole, do not believe that is glamorous. They have traveled enough to know that, beyond the county line, pork sausage links are slowly petrifying inside a stainless steel coffin over a chemical fire.

Still, I love to meet the people who read my work. I bear the sadist airlines. I man up to the talk shows. I once followed a dog that barked Christmas carols. I followed the guy who lost over two hundred pounds eating Subway sandwiches. Think about it.

But when I retire, it will be because I cannot stare down one more watery vat of unseasoned grits, one more begrimed hotel toaster. If I wanted to make my own toast, I'd stay at home, not stand here in line with America's future business leaders, a still-half-drunk wedding party, and an entire family reunion to use a toaster that shorted out in 1983.

Worst of all, though, is the abomination of the hotel biscuit. There is not enough congealing gravy in this world to cover the nastiness of a crunchy biscuit.

Fancy restaurants are no haven. At a four-star hotel, I had scrambled eggs that could have been used as packing material. At a bed-and-breakfast, I asked for bacon and eggs and got a strip of blackened bacon and a hockey-puck egg . . . and nothing else. This, in the South.

I guess we get what we settle for. I am always told I can order off the menu. The last time I did, they scooped it out of the buffet. I made my disgusted old man's face at them, but they are young and immune.

At least, soon, I can get the disgruntled, embittered old geezer discount.

Dangerous Games

⁓

I HAD PLANNED to spend my money in Pascagoula, Mississippi, maybe on some nice shrimp.

It was the car's fault that I didn't make it that far east. There I was, minding my own business, driving between New Orleans and Mobile, the Gulf shimmering green off my right shoulder, moving at about the same pace as the fat man in the bright blue bathing suit who was marching with great determination toward the slowly setting sun. I hummed that Jimmy Buffett song; you know the one.

> *Down around Biloxi*
> *Pretty girls are dancin'*

It was like the song had come to life around me. Little boys ran with plastic buckets, emptying the Gulf a half gallon at a time. I remember thinking: I should just find a place to park and feel the sun on my face.

But the car wanted to go to the casino. It made a hard left turn into a crowded parking lot and, like the Devil himself was clearing the way, steered itself into a space almost at the front entrance.

Well, I've learned you cannot argue with a Toyota . . . or the Devil, I suppose.

I strolled into the odd, glittering light—a thing that managed to be both gloom and glitz at the same time—and looked at the poker tables. If you're playing poker on a Sunday afternoon, you really care about it. The players had eyes like red-streaked marble; they looked at me the way my dog looks at a sausage biscuit.

I picked a less dangerous game, or at least I thought I had. I found a seat at a slot machine next to an old woman in a red pantsuit and a straw hat, one cigarette dangling from her lips and another one tucked behind her left ear.

She was losing pretty steadily, but I reckoned it would take awhile to eat up a house payment a nickel at a time. She jabbed the big plastic button with one knobby finger, and her fortunes spun and blurred and beeped. When I cleared my throat, to say hello, she fired a quick look at me that said all she needed to say.

Go away, you little @#&^% weasel.

I moved away. I decided to call her "Doris," because she looked like one. It's her own fault for being so surly, but that's just how a Doris will do you.

I found a machine without anyone near it and took a twenty from my wallet. The machine slurped it down, and then I stabbed the button. I got to hit it about forty times, which I think is around fifty cents a tap. Then it was just gone. Where did it go?

I grabbed another twenty and sent it into the machine, to go look for the other one. It was not successful, and I eased toward the exit.

"So long, Doris," I said as I passed. She did not look up.

Outside, the afternoon was dying, peaceful and slow. The Devil had ceased to be in possession of my Land Cruiser. I pointed it toward the state line, but I stayed on the coast, just because it is easy on the soul. Next time, I will just roll up two twenties, slip them in a bottle, and chuck it into the Gulf.

Maybe, if it comes back, it will be a hundred. I think the odds are about the same.

Driving Me Crazy

~~

I AM AFRAID my pickup truck is smarter than I am.

It used to be that a truck was just a truck, just an engine that left a little oil slick on the parking lot of the A&P. Mine had a transmission that growled like a dog every time I went from second to third and a radio that offered only AM and dead silence—if I could scrounge around on the floorboard amid the brake fluid cans and Grapico bottles to find the missing knob. I could, as a backup, spin the dial by carefully placing the blade of my pocketknife into the tiny slot on the post the knob was supposed to fit onto, but after stabbing myself a half-dozen times, I gave up.

Those trucks were as dumb as a pine knot. They were brutes, intended for hard, thankless manual labor, but at least they never made me feel intellectually inferior.

I got a new truck a few weeks ago for the same amount of money I spent on my first house. Even though I'm now in danger of debtors' prison, at least I can arrive there in style. Alabama does not actually have a debtors' prison, but at the rate we're going, it could happen any day. Maybe they'll just drive me over to our neighbor Georgia, which some say was founded as a penal colony. They have experience at that sort of thing. But I digress.

I settled on a truck that's so pretty people just stop and look at it in parking lots. At the dealership, I slid into the new leather and fired it up. The big V-8 engine rumbled, and we went down the blacktop in a glorious glide.

Glorious, till it began to lecture me.

Every time I strayed near the center line, it beeped me—and not one subtle *beep* but a loud, shrill, condescending alarm, as if just a split second of lost concentration were a mortal sin. I wrenched the wheel back in the other direction, and it lectured me again.

Now, understand, I was not creating carnage or cleaning out the ditches. I only strayed, just a little.

"I can live with this," I said to myself. But the more I tried to hold it dead-solid-perfect in the road, the more it weaved, until the truck, that harpy, was beeping more often than it wasn't. Finally, a warning light lit up the dashboard.

It showed a steaming cup of coffee and blinked the words—and I'm not making this up—"Perhaps you should take a break," or something to that effect. I think my truck thought I was sleepy, or maybe drunk. I expected it to shut off the engine and steer me to the curb. Instead, it beeped for another hundred miles and offered me, snobbishly, three dozen cups of coffee.

All in all, it is a fine truck. It's silvery blue with metal flakes and a dove-gray leather interior, and in the sun it even sparkles. You see, I can live with a truck that's prettier than I am. When I look in the mirror, not once has it flashed the words, "Son, you've really let yourself go. . . ."

The Best Part
of the Pig

Hands Off My Sandwich

⁓

WELL, THEY FINALLY MADE ME MAD.

I don't mind when they tell me that the way I talk is ador-able. I don't mind when they tell me, for the hundredth time, "That's not the way we do it up North." I don't even mind when they say our football teams are overrated, compared to Michigan and Notre Dame, which hasn't won a National Championship since practically the Hoover administration.

But when they start running down the tomato sandwich, that's all I can take. It never fails. At a talk or signing somewhere in the frozen tundra, someone will ask what we eat "down there," like I'm going to answer "dirt" or "bugs."

"A good tomato sandwich," I say.

"Tomato and what?" they always say.

"Just tomato, mayo, salt, and pepper, on white bread," I always say.

"Yuck," they always say. This should be a test for where the South begins. "Yuck" should tell us we have strayed too far toward the ice cap and should make a U-turn and not slow down until we see Spanish moss.

"I could understand," they say, "if you had some fresh romaine and a slice of good cheese and maybe some nice ham or turkey, maybe on pumpernickel."

"No," I say, "just tomato."

"Ugh," they say, which is even more insulting than "yuck."

I told this to Momma. "Some people," she said, "don't know what's good."

I grew up carrying tomato sandwiches in a paper sack to work or to the river to fish, wrapped in wax paper or in wrinkled, twice-used aluminum foil, which we treated like a precious metal. I guess because it was shiny.

The recipe was the same. Slather one thick slice of good white bread with real mayonnaise, and top with one or two thick slices of fresh tomato (late-summer ones are best) and salt and black pepper to taste—though the more pepper, the better. Top with another slice of white bread, slathered slightly less. It should not be soggy but still juicy in the middle.

"Yuck," they say.

There are things that seem delicious in your memory, but when you try to re-create them decades later, the taste is not what you believed, the way an old photograph will fade in time.

Nostalgia will trick you like that. Is it really the food, or the sun on your crew cut, or the mud between your toes? I don't know. But it's good enough.

I shouldn't care what they think, of course, but I fear they've convinced our children there's something wrong with us because we like these things. I once told a group of mostly Southern college students what I like to eat as a guilty pleasure. "A tomato sandwich, a pile of barbecue potato chips, and a frosty glass of whole milk," I said.

"Yuck," they said.

"Shut up," I said, silently reminding myself to give a C+ to them all.

Let's Eat Pig's Feet

I HAVE NEVER BEEN INCLINED to prove my pedigree by staring down a stalk of poke salad. I'm not tempted by a chitlin. I know what a chitlin does. It is said that my grandma worked eighteen hours to clean a chitlin, and it still smelled, in cooking, as if she were not altogether successful. I don't need a chitlin to be authentic.

I do not feel like I am betraying my culture by refusing squirrel brains. I do not feel I even need to defend myself on this.

"We ate 'em," my mother said, "but we were hungry."

I do not miss hog's head cheese. I remember walking into our kitchen once and seeing a hog's head lookin' at me.

I grew up with hog killings. I know you can't have a cracklin' or baked, crumbly hog jowl or fried potatoes or hot biscuits without them. But there was just something about the way that hog looked at me, like it knew something.

But some things call to me from the past. Pig's feet. Lord, I do miss them.

My mother eats them when I'm out of town. This is how old women will do you, if you made them mad once. They find out the things you enjoy, and cook them when you are over Salt Lake City.

When I told her some people were put off by pig's feet, she was mystified. "They cut the nail off," she said. I think she meant the hoof, but this is semantics.

All a pig's foot is, is the far south part of a ham, just another joint. It's succulent fat and cartilage. You can boil them, then pan roast them, till they all but melt off the knuckle, or—and this makes me happiest—you can pan barbecue them in a spicy, sweet, tomato-based sauce.

I must scrounge for them now, as they fade away. On the road, I scanned a thousand menus till I embarrassed myself with gratitude at Thomas Rib Shack in Tuscaloosa, Alabama. I had two of them, with good macaroni and cheese, yams, collards, and cornbread muffins. Once, I even had a pig's foot and a piece of fried chicken. I am not ashamed.

It is best not to take anything for granted. A few years ago, I walked into a little restaurant on State 59 between Robertsdale and Foley, Alabama, as they brought a tray of barbecued pig's feet out of the oven. I lingered, watching the sauce and clear fat from the feet mingle in the pan, and wondered if anyone would notice if I ate it with a spoon. I just ate it with my fingers. But the place went out of business, as if it had been a mirage.

I'm like an addict now, even rifling through my mother's home. I finally found where she hoards her pickled pig's feet, behind a row of canned corn we bought by the ton at the dollar store.

Conscience prevailed, and I went to the store to get my own. There was only a dusty ring on the shelf. I blame the squeamish, and the young, and the posers, talkin' about Roy Acuff with gelato on their breath.

But like that spooky hog, I know.

Home of the Po'Boy

CAN YOU REMEMBER the happiest you've ever been? I am not talking about the birth of a child, or finding religion, or anything to do with a lottery ticket or go-go boots. I guess that would be Big Happy. I am talking about being a little happy, being glad in your own skin, for one modest moment in time.

I can remember.

It was on Annunciation Street. It was almost a decade ago, not long after I returned to my little shotgun double in Uptown New Orleans from a life sentence in an ice-bound gulag—really just two weeks covering the Winter Olympics in Salt Lake City. I was homesick, and hungry. Dodging potholes so old and deep that the Devil must use them as a shortcut home, I bounced down Annunciation Street to a place called Domilise's Po-Boy and Bar.

Inside, a cadre of no-nonsense ladies were spreading sizzling fried shrimp on perfect French bread, then dressing them in shredded lettuce with just enough mayonnaise and a drizzle of red sauce (ketchup, hot sauce, and white magic). No tomatoes. You cannot get good tomatoes all the time in New Orleans, so the beloved Dot Domilise, who has passed on, banned them. "They kinda get in the way," she once told me. The shrimp were perfect, not too big, not too small. "If they're too small," she said, "you just get the crust."

I took my sandwich, with a cold Barq's root beer, to an ancient table. I looked at it for a minute, thinking how odd that anyone would call such a lustrous thing a "po'boy." Then, I took a bite. I cannot tell you how it tasted; my dictionary only has words coined by mortal men. But that was one damn good sandwich.

People love this old city for many reasons, for music and architecture, of course, and some for the fact that they can careen dang near naked down Bourbon Street one night and then go home to Indiana and sell life insurance. But for me, when I come back to this city, I am happiest in the company of a po'boy.

They are iconic now, like red beans. People argue over who has the best, but there are so many places and so many recipes—from fried oysters to roast beef, barbecued shrimp to catfish, soft-shell crab to hot smoked sausage—that picking one is like feeling around in a sack of rubies.

I am not a native and have not lived here for a long time, and if I am a food critic, I am a fat Italian opera singer. I volunteered to write this story about po'boys so I could return to New Orleans and eat some more. But there is something strange about them. You hold one in your hands and you feel like a native, the same way, when I hold a fine Cuban sandwich in Miami, I think I can speak Spanish. Hand me a fried oyster po'boy, and I catch myself muttering, "Oh, y'ah, babe," and such as that.

People here still discuss, sometimes loudly, how the sandwiches got their name, but perhaps the most popular story dates back to the flames and flying bricks of the city's streetcar strike in '29. Two brothers, Clovis and Benjamin Martin, gave striking transit workers free sandwiches—said to be made from debris from roast beef on French bread—at their restaurant on St. Claude Avenue. When a hungry striker walked up, workers there would shout that another poor boy was at the door. And if that's not the truth, it ought to be. People are always finding new po'boys, fancier ones, but I do not pretend to be on a voyage of discovery for a foie gras po'boy or one stuffed with quail's eggs.

For me, Domilise's will always be queen. The sandwiches constructed in the small restaurant were so consistently fine that once a group of writers made a pact not to mention the restaurant in stories about New Orleans in fear that Domilise's, like so many neighborhood jewels, would be overrun by tourists who would not know the difference between a po'boy and a pineapple upside-down cake. That secret, if it ever was one, has long since gotten out.

The first time I walked in there—the first thing you see are those ladies cooking—I almost apologized and backed out. People like to say that walking into a family restaurant is like walking into someone's kitchen, but there you do.

I once asked Dot where she went if she wanted a po'boy.

"There's good places," she said, "you know, in other neighborhoods."

For many people in New Orleans, the best po'boy—a direct descendant of the '29 sandwich—is roast beef, but lavish now, shaved thin, piled high, and smothered in brown gravy. How much gravy? One New Orleans resident once said it's not enough unless, when you hold the sandwich over your head, the gravy runs halfway down your arm.

Terri Troncale, the statuesque former editorial page editor at *The Times-Picayune,* does not require that much, but concedes, in this city of excess, she has never encountered a dry sandwich. Her favorite roast beef is found not far from Bayou St. John in Mid-City, at a place called Parkway Bakery & Tavern.

"It tastes like my momma's pot roast. Wonderful," says Troncale. The roast beef is tender, the gravy just right, permeating the bread. The taste builds a bridge in her memories. With that first bite, "I think about my momma."

In my own failing memory, I can build whole days around a po'boy. Once, when a friend was sanding the floors of his shotgun double, I volunteered to go get lunch—driving being preferable to sanding, and much better than sweeping. I was in a backed-up line at a fast-food hamburger joint when it struck me: I was in New Orleans, and I was simmering here, in exhaust fumes, to get a bad hamburger.

I fled to the tiny Guy's Po-Boys on Magazine Street for some sandwiches to go, planning on a couple of simple ham and cheese po'boys. But there on the menu was the most ridiculous thing: pork chop po'boys. I think I might have clapped my chubby little hands together like a child.

I ordered two pork chop po'boys, grilled, dusted with cayenne, and dressed with lettuce, tomato, and mayo. I grabbed two root beers and some Zapp's potato chips. Zapp's, made down here, are to regular chips what a shot of Jim Beam is to warm milk. The sandwiches came wrapped in clean white butcher paper, a foot long. We ate them on the stoop, and I cannot recall a word we said; could be we never said much to remember, anyway. But I can still see the stoop of that fine old house, still see the cast-aside white butcher paper, redolent of mayonnaise, still smelling of grilled pork. I remember thinking: *Wonder if anybody would notice if I licked that?*

If I were a sandwich, I think, I would be a po'boy, overstuffed, a little sloppy, relatively cheap, and bad for you—and, as often as in reality, wearing gravy someplace on me. But two of my favorite po'boys do not really resemble—or pretend to be—po'boys at all.

Casamento's Restaurant on Magazine may be one of the most unusual restaurants I have ever seen. The interior is covered in gleaming tile and, in a city that can sometimes shrug off niceties for the sake of great food, is eerily clean. It is only open in the cooler months, which down here is a relative term. But its sandwiches are worth waiting on.

Its oyster loaf is filled with some of the finest such creatures I have ever encountered, delicately covered in corn flour and fried in an honest-to-God iron skillet. They are served on thick slabs of white bread, not the airy French bread or more chewy Cajun bread. And that, oysters and bread and maybe a taste of butter, is all you need here. I love my condiments, but this would only tart up perfection.

At Liuzza's by the Track, the barbecued shrimp po'boy has a legend of its own. It is barbecued only in the New Orleans sense, meaning that shrimp are cooked in butter and spices, then stuffed into hollowed-out bread and drenched in the buttery liquid from the skillet. I ate as much as I could and wore the rest home on the front of my shirt, and I am not ashamed. I had heard about this sandwich so long from so many people that, when I finally went to the restaurant, I was afraid that it—like Bigfoot—did not really exist. Drowned by Katrina, Liuzza's rose from several feet of water with its legends, and menu, intact.

There are a dozen, two dozen more good sandwiches, slowly crumbling in my memories. But one I never got to try. Dirt-common in New Orleans, it is the french fry po'boy, slopped over with brown gravy and dressed with mayonnaise, lettuce, and tomato.

You can make a face if you want. But you know you want one, too.

Don't Mess with the Recipe

～)

THEY CHANGED THE NAME not long ago from Roma's to Nick's Place, to honor the restaurant's longtime patriarch, but most of the people huddled over their hamburger steaks still call it Roma's and will call it that till they die. We hold on to things here. Another local landmark—a beautiful lake—dried up decades ago, but the street sign still reads Nisbet Lake Road.

Some amount of change may be inevitable here in Jacksonville, Alabama, but until someone messes with the recipe for the Thousand Island dressing, my people will come to this place, rest their bones in the Naugahyde booths, and watch the world and the pickup trucks spin around the city square—which is more of a circle, really—in my hometown.

We used to have other places, but they have since faded into memory. Call them meat 'n' threes or mom-and-pop shops or whatever you like. They're vanishing, which is unacceptable. I have watched the days of my life roll by in the window-front booth at Roma's. I count on the scenes, smells, and tastes to keep these remaining days of mine somehow on level.

I wrote my first story on a manual typewriter in the dark office of the nearby *Jacksonville News* and then celebrated my rise to fame as a big shot writer over a sirloin steak sandwich at Roma's.

It put a dent in my salary of fifty dollars a week, but how do you celebrate with a Happy Meal?

Little has changed. Miz Tina, the matriarch who gives me homemade bread to take to my mother, still sits at a corner table, surrounded by family and friends, snapping a great pile of green beans. Miz Sophie, in the kitchen, will prepare them the next day with chicken, sweet potatoes, and macaroni and cheese. A grandchild, Konstantina, spends part of the day in Miz Tina's lap and part of it whirling through the joint. The waitress, Carolina, asks me if I want the usual or the special.

Not much else is necessary.

Bland, impersonal food has become acceptable in many places—but not here. My junior high school basketball coach sits in one booth. (He paddled me once for wrestling on the basketball court.) The boy I was wrestling with sits three booths away. Nostalgia, and the food, hold us.

It is the same across the state in Northport, at an institution called Mr. Bill's Southern Smokehouse, where the chicken breast is crisp and the coleslaw is made fresh. There are hearing aids in every fifteenth seat; old folks will not eat bad food. Now their children and grandchildren come. They were raised right.

It's the same at Saraceno's Restaurant in Fairhope, where the family-run buffet has corn casserole and potatoes—and if the Baptists get in front of you on a Sunday, you can die of anticipation. The town's great hallmark, Ben's Jr. Bar-B-Que, closed recently; it leaves a cold place here.

But about three hundred miles to the north, the grill at Roma's remains hot to the touch, hot enough to warm a lifetime—and a town.

Savor the Bread Pudding Soufflé
at Commander's Palace

⁓

HERE, EVEN THE EARTH UNDER YOUR FEET is not a given, a certainty. In drought, New Orleans turned to powder, to something like an old woman's Bruton snuff, and the piers that held up the shotgun doubles would sink into the earth. For those of us not born here, the first thing you asked, when you went to buy a house, was not the price, but whether it was at least somewhat level. I took a marble, once, to test it. It took off like a shot. In rain, so far below sea level, you think not about puddles, but the End of Days.

You could not, here, count on the absolute of time. A ten-minute ride from the Quarter to Uptown could take your natural life if there was a parade. You could not count on the streetcar. Whole student bodies at Loyola matriculated while the torn-up tracks were a promise and a precious memory.

But you could count on a lot that made up for it. You could count on a good po'boy on Annunciation Street, and good coffee anywhere. You could count on fine piano on the radio. You could count, if you lived near a supermarket, on little old ladies leaving their carts in your front yard, or against the bumper of your Pontiac. You could count on a pork chop sandwich, and, if dressed with extra mayonnaise, count on needing a new shirt.

Still, if what they say is true, if a perfect moment in this old city really can last a lifetime, then I guess you can count on one fine dessert, and a first spoonful that always seems to surprise, even if you have looked forward to it for months or even years.

The first time I had the Creole bread pudding soufflé with warm whiskey cream at Commander's Palace, I counted on quite a bit. Any dessert you almost have to order before you hand over your hat? It must be one hell of a thing.

It was. The only dessert I had in life that compared was my momma's sweet dumplings, and if it were not for hurting her feelings, I would be more profound. I can say that the closest I came to passing out here had nothing to do with Jim Beam in the old Pontchartrain Hotel, but from joy. People from my part of Alabama do not use the word "heavenly," but I would if I could.

The dessert is made, I hear from people smarter than me, by folding meringue into custard made with bread from the Leidenheimer Baking Company and flavored with simple things like vanilla, cinnamon, raisins, and such. It comes as a poufy dome in a soufflé cup, whatever that is, and I was just beginning to be a little uncomfortable when the waiter poked a hole in the dome with a silver spoon and ladled in the whiskey sauce. The place could charge five dollars just to let you smell it.

There was more substance inside than I thought, and I ate all I could scrape away, down to a line of sugar glued to the rim of the soufflé cup. I hope, at least, no one was looking.

Usually, it is hard to rediscover, or renew, a perfect moment. But I will count on it, unless there is a parade.

Louisiana Food

IT MAY BE THE MAGIC IS REAL. Here amid marked-down voo-
doo and dime-store gris-gris, between piney woods preachers
and deep swamp fortune-tellers, may swirl real spirits that enrich
this place, or at least permeate the food that delights us and drinks
that lubricate us. Here, where something as humble as a wooden
spoon can seem like a magic wand, where ghosts of ancestors stir
a little something extra into recipes passed down 150 years, things
routinely taste better than the chemistry of ingredients or the
alchemy of preparation should allow. I tasted it for the first time
more than a quarter century ago, swirling up and into and through
me, from the bottom of a glass.

It was on the balcony of the Columns Hotel on St. Charles Avenue. I was sitting in a wicker chair, just decrepit enough to be comfortable, drinking a glass of Jim Beam on the rocks. I am not a big
drinker, but there was always something comforting about brown
liquor. After one, I always felt like I was covered in a warm quilt.
The secret, across my life and my ancestors' lives, was not to drink
seven more, turn the quilt into a cape or a parachute, and jump off
something tall.

This time I only had the one. I was down to ice and watered-
down whiskey—wasn't it Sinatra who said you had to let it lay in

the ice a little while?—when that special peace slipped over and around me, but in a way I had never felt before. The old streetcar, the color of a World War II surplus jeep, clanked and rattled on the neutral ground below with a rhythm I had never heard. From the bar below, a smell of candied cherries and orange slices and spiced rum and good perfume seemed to reach up and out into the dusk around me. The live oaks creaked. The night flowed through the ancient trees like a river. And I could have slept, if that glass had held just one half inch more. I sipped the last of the liquor—the same liquor you can buy in almost any bar in this world—and my mind emptied for a just a few precious minutes of contention and ambition, and filled with the essence of this place, this street, this city, this state. And all the conjurer behind the bar had to do was unscrew a bottle, and pour.

Think of the magic that Celestine Dunbar and her family created in their place on Freret Street, before the waters took it: fried seafood platters that came so fast from the fryer that you could scorch your hands and fried chicken that made grown men damn near cry, served with stewed okra, and sweet potato pies, and good cornbread. You could eat all the barbecued chicken and stewed cabbage you could stand on a weekday, give the nice lady at the cash register ten dollars and have enough left to tip like a sultan, ride the streetcar and buy a grape snow cone. The allure of that fried chicken held me so tightly that after the city drowned I traced it to Loyola, where Mrs. Dunbar would make young people the best lunch in the whole academic world—many of whom had no idea from whence the source of that magic came. I have forgotten most of the food I have eaten in this life. I have never forgotten one crumb of hers.

I know cynics will say it is just cooking. Maybe. I mean, how complicated is this food, really? You simmer some beans, roast some fat hog, boil some shrimps or some blue crabs, concoct some gumbo. You have been taught, over generations, not to fear the salt shaker, or the butter, or the garlic, and you do not sprinkle cayenne so much as you ladle it. You give onions, green pepper, and celery a celestial name, to raise them above the mundane of simple ingredients, but it is still just seasoning.

But how do you explain the difference in grabbing lunch elsewhere in this poor ol' sorry world to sitting down to a plate of creamy red beans and roasted ham shank at Betsy's Pancake House on Canal Street, where the fat from the meat slowly, slowly drips down to season the already perfectly seasoned beans, as much like other beans as a Tiffany necklace is like a string of old beads left in a tree. How do you explain how anything—anything—served on a melamine plate with a side of potato salad can rival meals you have paid two hundred dollars to enjoy, and, if you were true to yourself, you would actually rather have the plate of beans? For the rest of my life, I will remember watching my teenage stepson devour a plate of Betsy's beans and smoked sausage without taking time to talk or apparently even breathe, then announce that he really, really wanted to go to school in New Orleans. He lived the first sixteen years of his life on chicken fingers and cheese pizza. But he knew magic when he tasted it.

It is the same outside the city, from corner to corner, pocket to pocket, in this state. You can even be hexed in a Holiday Inn.

In Gonzales, just off the interstate and affixed to a chain hotel, is a Mike Anderson's restaurant that prepares a crawfish bisque that is nothing like the chalky, fake mess most places prepare. It is a rich, brown stew, redolent—I have always liked to say "redolent"—with onions, bell pepper, crawfish tails that do not taste like they came from a hold of an oceangoing freighter, and crawfish heads stuffed with a dressing that is best devoured by fishing it out with a crooked finger. Local people—not just tourists and weary travelers—pile in by the carload on weekend nights, proof that it is not just the visual or sensual appeal of this state that fools us into thinking things taste better here.

Sometimes, though, the spell this place casts settles around me so completely that I wonder if I can ever leave it and eat the way regular people eat. It happened in the warmth of a corner table at The Upperline in New Orleans, on something as humble as cornbread. But here the sweet cornbread came topped with grilled, spiced shrimp, and shaved purple onions, and something that looked like rich folks' mayonnaise but I now think might have been some kind of potion. They only gave me two little squares, about six bites in all. I looked at the empty plate with such awful regret, thinking, If I had just taken smaller bites . . .

I forgot, after a bite or two, that I was bound up like an asylum inmate in my too-tight sport coat, forgot every warning my doctor ever gave, forgot that when you leave this place there are potholes of doom ready to swallow you whole and daiquiri-dazed drivers waiting to run you down. You forget everything here, in this Louisiana, for a spoonful. If that is not magic, I by God don't know what magic is.

Why Nothing Beats
a Classic Southern Diner

⁓

SOMETIMES, YOU JUST NEED TO SIT in a corner booth at about two or three o'clock in the afternoon, still trying to wake up good, surrounded by the rising plumes of Marlboros, and have a good breakfast.

I am not talking about a hangover breakfast; I am too old for that foolishness. I am talking about a Tuesday.

I am a late sleeper; nothing good has ever happened to me before noon. If the phone rings, it is bad news, or a telemarketer in Sri Lanka apprising me of my refrigerator warranty. If my alarm goes off, it means the Atlanta airport, or Interstate 59, or doctors. All surgeries occur in a gray dawn; I had a kidney stone retrieval once at seven a.m., which was just mean. I think I might even have more religion, if it were not for timing; I spoke at a prayer breakfast once and am still largely unaware what I said.

So I decided to just write off mornings. If I wake up at 11:59, I go back to bed; a lot of misery could happen between then and 12.

I did, after a while, kind of get to missing breakfast.

Thank you, Huddle House, for setting the world back to spinning, once more.

I cannot speak for all outposts, but the one in Jacksonville, Alabama, is a reason to live. It is not just the fact you can get a fine Western omelet as the sun begins its downhill slide, that the grits pot is always bubbling, or that sausage gravy is considered an acceptable accoutrement to, say, a chef salad.

It is that all this exists in a wider time warp. You hear a lot of philosophy here, one bacon, egg, and cheese biscuit at a time, and hear a lot of wisdom that is rapidly going out of style.

This is one of the last places l know where gray-haired old men do not talk politics or football but reminisce about work, of third shift at Goodyear or the pipe shop or a life swinging on a ladder with a paint bucket in their hand. Old women talk about machines at the cotton mill that like to took their life, and how ol' so-and-so at the beauty shop ought to have her license taken away after the way she burnt up their momma's hair. And she was just goin' in for a *curl*.

You learn that Dodge makes a good diesel, and it is okay to cry over a good dog.

The waitresses know everyone's name, their order, more. The old men try to flirt with them, but not very well, as they go through a Camel or three waiting for their Smokehouse Platter or just their twelfth cup of coffee. It is one of the last smoker-friendly restaurants around—maybe the last—though that is changing, I am told, with a planned remodel. I am not a smoker, so it will be easier on me; I won't have to dread every person who walks in, or worry they will sit down next to me and fire up a stogie as long as a Philly Cheese. But that is as much change as I am willing to allow. I'd rather choke down some blue haze than lose that wisdom.

How else will I know who quit drinking, or who got saved, and who is stealing boat motors on Lake Wedowee?

Later, Gator

I DO NOT EAT ALLIGATOR. I know I will offend many alligator-eating bon vivants, but I will not eat anything that tastes like an unholy union between a fish and a chicken. To me, it tastes like the lizard it is, and I will not eat lizard just to be picturesque. I ate some alligator in Louisiana once that I said I liked at the time, but after much time and careful consideration I believe I might have been less than sincere.

But, mostly, I choose not to eat alligators because they did not eat me.

I was reminded of it, not long ago. I was on a muddy bayou near Mobile Bay. I saw an alligator looking at me like I was a Boston butt.

I don't know how big he was. I could only see the bumps of his eyes and the tip of his snout showing above the water, inscrutable, you know, the way alligators can be.

But I know what he was thinking.

Yeah, you just wander a little bit closer over here, big boy, and let's see if you get lucky again.

Some alligators tried to eat me, once. I made it easy for them.

I was on Lake Okeechobee, about twenty-five years ago. I remember it was one of those nights that only happen in inland Florida. The air was thick with mosquitoes *and* raindrops, buzzing, fluttering in my ears, biting through my wet clothes. We glided in two boats through the lake's rim canal, and the black water glowed with the orange-red eyes of modern-day dragons.

I fell out of the boat, in eighteen feet of water. No, I was not drunk, though when my people fall out of a boat they usually are. I was jumping from one boat to another, during a legal alligator hunt, and did not do that with any great success. I jumped short, banged onto the side of the boat, and *ka-woosh!* It actually made that sound. *Ka-woosh!* I was going to die, I thought, to the sound of a flushing toilet.

I sank like a sack of lead sinkers but, failing to drown, surfaced into a nightmare. All around me, in every direction I looked, were those eyes, reflecting in the flashlight beams that swept the surface of the lake.

Gators. Big gators. The same gators we had been trying to stab all night with a steel harpoon.

I do not know if gators actually hold a grudge—I hear their brains are very, very small—but I suspect they could remember being molested with a harpoon. I hung there for several long minutes at the side of the boat, neck-deep, water-logged, unable to pull myself back into the boat, thinking, at any second, I would feel the jaws close on me.

I have no doubt they *would* have eaten me, if I had dawdled just a little bit longer. I finally clawed my way back up over the transom to safety, and went limp, rain in my face, dirty water and skeeters in my nose. There are photographs.

I went on other alligator hunts in my life, but stayed my behind in the boat. Still, they had their chance at me, more than once, and I remain uneaten.

So, I will not eat them. Of course, that is easy to say. Neither will I eat chitlins, or dirt.

I wonder sometimes, what I would do, if gator tasted like beef short ribs, or barbecued shrimp.

I think I would go back to Okeechobee, with a harpoon.

Relations

Fishing for the Moon

I HAVE A THOUSAND THINGS I wanted to do.

I wanted to catch a fine blue marlin, or a swordfish, or maybe a big tarpon, but I fear I might be too feeble to do so without help, and that would be like not catching one at all. I used to want to drive a fine Italian sports car; I used to, but now my reflexes are so bad I would just drive it into a ditch. I'd just have to sit in one, and go "vroom, vroom."

I wanted to run away to Wyoming, or maybe New Mexico, and ride a tall horse across a wide and open space, and wear a big hat, and chase the buffalo. But the thing about a tall horse is that it's a long way from the ground, and I am brittle now, and it would hurt too much when I hit the ground.

I wanted to do a lot of things—some I did once, and others were only dreams. Most are unrealistic now. But not everything. Once more, I'd like to fly a kite.

I think of it every March, on those days when the sun is bright and yellow and the wind blows in my face, hard enough to make a sound in the trees still bare from the winter. When I was a child, in elementary school, the teacher read us poems about March winds, and what good is a wind without a sail, or a kite? To me, with a little imagination, they were the same thing.

We made them from thin sticks and old newspaper, and I flew *The Anniston Star* proudly across the blue sky. We cut and pieced a tail from quilt scraps, all of it amounting to a feat of aerodynamic engineering that I couldn't repeat now, no matter how hard I tried. I know it, somehow, the way I know my hands are too big for the gloves I wore in second grade. But in 1966, I was a kite-building fool.

Later, after I begged long and hard, my mother bought me a kite with the skull and crossbones of the Jolly Roger printed on its front, and I would lie in the tall broom sedge near Germania Springs, stare into the blue sky, and dream about great battles throughout the Spanish Main.

A lifetime later, a friend of my father's, Jack, told me that he and my father did the same when they were boys, and built a kite so sturdy and perfect it flew out of sight. And when another boy ambled up and asked what they were doing holding to that string that seemed to vanish into thin air, my daddy said, "We're fishing." And when the boy asked what for, my daddy told him, "Why, for the man in the moon."

Every March, I think I might like to fly one again. I think I might like to find an open space, free of what Charlie Brown called those kite-eating trees, and see if—at the very least—I can get the thing off the ground. My imagination, and my dreams, may be a little worn, too, but now I have memories to send aloft. It may not seem like much to you, but it beats falling off a horse.

Why Momma Loves Me Anyway

FOR HALF A CENTURY, I have failed at getting my mother a thoughtful gift for Mother's Day.

I thought, as I stared at the pitiful condition of her kitchen's screened door, I had found a thing that could not miss. It was not just that the screened door could no longer keep out the flies; I was not altogether certain a turkey buzzard, or a pterodactyl, could not glide through. I headed for the hardware store, but I didn't even make it out of the driveway before my conviction came apart like that raggedy door.

You might think Mother's Day would be easy for me. I have written about her for three decades and should have her figured out. But in all that time, the only truly adequate gift I have given her was two grocery bags full of pork fat, but that is another story. One hit in a thousand clear misses.

I got her a classic, two-tone blue 1956 Chevrolet. She used it as a greenhouse. I got her a house. It had too many lightbulbs. I got her another. The driveway is too steep. I got her false teeth.

She spit them out in the weeds, just outside Pell City, Alabama.

It all failed. Jewelry is frivolous. Cute stuff and doodads gather dust twelve-deep on the windowsills. "How many piggy banks," she asked me once, "does a poor woman need?" Cut flowers sometimes made her sad; live flowers required digging a hole.

Finally, I decided to sit down with a No. 2 pencil and list the things I knew she enjoyed.

This amounted to good coffee, snuff, Westerns, and TV preachers who preach the Full Gospel and have excellent piano players. She is, as we have written here, also fond of mariachis.

I crossed them off one by one. You will pay hell getting a mariachi to do a command performance at the end of our driveway, and I am pretty sure I cannot afford a TV preacher. Westerns, then? I considered DVDs—which she calls "them little round things"—of her favorites, but that would require teaching her to use the DVD player, and there is no time for that, she said, before the Lord comes back.

Snuff, then? And coffee? She said I was wasting money, and it was a sin to waste it on such vices.

"They're YOUR vices," I said.

But that door, now, that door needed to be replaced. But first, I asked her. I should have known better.

"Can't," she said.

"Why?" I said.

"The cats," she said.

"What do the cats have to do with it?" I said.

"The cats tore it up in the first place, hangin' on it. It would be foolish to get them a nice, brand-new door, just to hang on and tear it up like they've done."

The terrifying thing is, she kind of made sense.

I decided to give her money. I heard she spent it on snuff and coffee.

Along for the Ride

～

SHE DOES NOT BURN UP THE ROADS ANYMORE. We took a trip the other day—she, my mother, and I—and made it all the way to the Coosa backwater. Nothing was as we remembered. The old roads were overgrown or covered in four lanes, and we got lost going to places we did not even know we were going to. Still, it was a fine trip. We got an Icee and stayed out after dark. But once, long ago, you should have seen her go.

Because of her, I know what the squish of river mud feels like between my toes. Without her, I never would have walked through Little Jerusalem. I never would have seen Rome . . . Georgia. I never would have seen the blast furnaces set the sky ablaze over Birmingham, or had a Big Mac in the back seat just the other side of Montgomery. Oh, I would have seen it all, eventually, but it needed to happen to a boy; the world loses much of its wonder about the time you pay your first water bill.

I don't think I ever thanked my Aunt Juanita, for taking me along.

The first big trip was usually around the first of June, when hateful school came to a close. You watched the clock that last day, but even the hot air seemed stuck in place, composed mostly of chalk dust and floor wax, thick and still. Finally, after a math class so long it defied any numerical configuration, the last bell of the school year sent a stampede of cowlicks and brogans out into a brand-new summer, clean, fresh, and free. And there, behind the wheel of a beige Chevrolet Biscayne, clutch pushed down, patting the gas, was my Aunt Juanita.

With my mother riding shotgun, she would show us as much of the world as two tanks of regular would allow. I can still see her that way, in dime-store flip-flops, one bony elbow out the open window. I do not recall a map.

"Don't no moss grow on that woman," the old men liked to say, and now that I am old and sophisticated, I know there is a word for the way she was. My Aunt Juanita was born with a case of wanderlust, a need to feel the blacktop whirring beneath those recapped tires.

We rode and rode, wedged in there with inner tubes and lapdogs and softly snoring grandmas, and dined on Grapico sodas and Golden Flake Cheese Curls and melting black walnut ice cream. On long trips, like the three-hundred-mile exodus to the Gulf, we devoured fried chicken and cold biscuits from aluminum foil, four doors flung open under Spanish moss. On short trips, we stopped for tomato sandwiches and cans of Vienna sausages.

We thought that was as good as life might ever be. It might have been.

She is eighty-three now. She wants to go up near Summerville, Georgia, soon to visit the graves of some kin. On the way, maybe I can get her a Grapico, and tell her what it all meant to me.

Kitchen-Sink Curls

⁓

EVERY AUGUST, as the heat of another Alabama summer settles upon the land, I'm haunted by the memories . . . no, the
horrors . . . of the lingering scent of drugstore chemicals and the
terrifying sight of unnaturally curly hair.

We are, for the most part, a people of straight hair. My Aunt
Jo had some curls when she was little, but we were, and still are,
a lank-haired family. We always looked upon curly-headed folks
with envy. Their hair did not lie flat on their foreheads and necks,
plastered there with sweat.

They looked—I don't know—kind of springy. Breezy, almost.

I had my momma's hair. It was as straight as a Lutheran and had
the consistency of a spiderweb.

In drier, cooler weather, the static electricity would make it
point toward the moon. I didn't know till I was about six or so that
there was actually a remedy for this.

Wealthier women went to a place called the beauty shop and
had their hair rolled and processed and then baked under what
seemed to be a big, round toaster oven, usually as they talked
about who might be with child.

Women like my mother performed this mystical procedure
right in their kitchens. "Go outside and play," she always told me.
"Momma's gonna get her a permanent."

"A perm'nent what?" I asked.

"Go," she ordered.

The procedure was too complicated, and obviously danger-ous, to be performed alone. One of my aunts usually assisted, first draping my mother with what appeared to be a plastic bedsheet.

So, I mused, it must be some kind of surgery.

I'd later learn that I was barred from the house because of the fumes. They'd practically knock flies from the air in that hot, un-air-conditioned little space.

After what seemed to be most of an afternoon, it was over, and I'd hear her call us at suppertime. People joke about how far a mother's voice will carry, across the pines and the cotton fields. I know that's a scientific fact. I'd rate her range at about three miles.

I remember running for the house with great anticipation. Sup-per was the best time of day every day, and if you got there first, you got the chicken leg or the delicious little cube of pork swim-ming in the pinto beans.

The sight of Momma almost caused me to choke on my drooling tongue. Her blond hair had been transformed into a round hel-met of tight, alien curls, and it all smelled more than a little like Monsanto.

"Eek!" I said—I really did.

"Looks good, Momma," lied my brother Sam as he wagged a chicken leg in front of my face.

Now, more than a half century later, I still do not know why it was called a permanent, since it certainly was not. In a few days, the curls would begin to go away. In a month or so, it was as straight as a board, and she looked like my momma again.

Maybe they called it a permanent because of the duration of the psychological scarring. I don't know.

In time, I ceased to envy people with curls. Now I envy those with hair of any kind.

Mariachi Momma

～っ

SHE FOUND SOME JOY, next to the guacamole.
Let me explain.

I have the same worries as all people with elderly parents. Will my mother take her medicine, or decide she should ingest her blood pressure pills only when the moon is full? Will she watch her sugar, or continue to tell me that a Krispy Kreme doughnut is fine as long as she eats only the outside? "Hon, the inside, that doughy part, is bad for you." Will she watch her step on her walks, or will she go skating down the hill on a rocket sled of slick leaves, then tell me, three days later, she fell down? But you figure on such. Things happen.

Now, I have to worry about her running off with the mariachis. Let me explain further. I talked my mother and little brother, Mark, into eating at a good Mexican restaurant in Fairhope, Alabama, on a Monday night. They had never eaten at one before, and if you find this hard to believe, you probably have never been south of Houston Street. I did, in fact, once take my mother to a bad Mexican restaurant in North Alabama, but it was about as Mexican as a fjord. She dragged her fork across a microwaved enchilada fabricated from Play-Doh, swore I was trying to kill her, and fled.

But this place in Fairhope—called, imaginatively, El Mexicano—was a fine, warm, comfortable place, always full, always savory, and dependable. We sat down, and the waiter was sweet to my mother, as he was to all *abuelas*. She ate salsa and pronounced it tasty, and relished the guacamole, which she told me "is real good for you." She was digging into a chile relleno and a cheese-and-onion enchilada when the air was rent by a bloodcurdling . . .

"Aieeeeeeeeeeeeee!" Trumpets sounded. Guitars rang.

Three men in tight, spangly pants walked into the room, strumming on guitars as big as johnboats, and began to sing loudly in Spanish a song I did not know, but that did not mean it wasn't fine. An elderly woman at the table next to us—someone's *abuela,* I'll bet—got up and danced, got up and shook it right there among the chimichangas. I prepared to call the ambulance for my mother, who I feared would pass out. Mariachi Monday, I thought to myself. I had plumb forgotten.

My mother is not the kind of woman who likes a marching band with her entrée. I started to apologize to her, just before the band shifted, smoothly, into a Spanish and English version of "I'll Fly Away," then "Sweet Home Alabama" in Español.

"Why, it's just beautiful," she said, and she meant it. She hung on every song, her food forgotten. The mariachis, men in their fifties, moved to our table to take a request. I consulted with my mother, and we asked for an old favorite.

> But if he ever breaks your heart
> If the teardrops ever start

I don't like clichés, but there's no avoiding it here. My mother hung on every word.

As we left, she stood in the door, lingering, lingering. "I guess we've got to go," I said, but we didn't, and stayed a few more minutes.

I do not believe my mother would really run off with the mariachis. She has thirteen cats. But I may get her a sombrero, for her birthday.

Who's in Charge Here?

❧

I WORRY ABOUT MY MOMMA all the time. I realize the whole world is, at this moment, worrying about their mommas. Half are wondering if they took their blood pressure medicine; the other half are busy wondering if a telemarketer sold them a time-share in Florida. At least three of us are just wondering if our mommas unplugged the coffeepot.

One day a year—this month—we celebrate them, and if we're lucky enough to have them with us on this earth, we send flowers and take them to the buffet at the Western Sizzlin'. The other 364 days, we worry that they'll trip over the dog. It is what the children talk about when we gather in secret to share our misery.

"Momma just won't do right," someone will sigh.

"Well, she's just headstrong, the dear," someone else will reply.

"Mm-hmm," everyone else will say, in chorus.

"Are you talkin' about me?" a momma will shout from across the house. They can't hear a lick when you ask them about their blood sugar, but whisper something about them and suddenly they have bat ears.

I have friends who say how strange it is to take care of their parents after all these years, for roles to reverse. They should live in my house.

There is no role reversal, because that would require me to be mature and responsible.

Instead, everyone here is running with scissors. I asked her, in good faith, if she was eating well. "Yes," she lied.

"What are you eating?" I asked.

"A pineapple sandwich on white bread with mayonnaise," she replied.

"You've got to eat better," I said.

"Do you want one?" she asked.

"Sure," I answered.

She told me recently that her toe hurt. "Well," I said, "we have to take you to the toe doctor."

"Can't," she said.

"Why?" I asked.

"Don't like him," she said.

"Which one?" I asked.

"None of 'em," she said. I had no argument for this. So I told her that her toe would fall off, and when it did, she'd better not come crying to me.

When I do get her to an appointment, she loudly gives her opinion on doctors in general.

She assigns them names. Her dermatologist, for instance, is Dr. Butcher.

And so we go. I try to get her to do right for a while, but I always give in eventually—I guess because doing right is still such a mystery to me. This past Mother's Day, I asked her what she wanted. "Some Red Diamond coffee," she requested. I gave her about ten pounds of it, a can of crushed pineapple, and some pickled pig's feet. Someone has to be the grown-up around here.

Why I Write About Home

~⌒

I WRITE ABOUT HOME so I can be certain that someone will. It is not much more complicated than that.

Home for me has always been as much a matter of class as location. My home is not the comfortable South, not the big churches, or the country clubs, or the giant waterfront houses on the lakes, or the columned mansions on the main drags.

Home for me is not a skybox at Alabama or Auburn, or good seats at Turner Field in Atlanta. It is not even the Kiwanis Club, or the Rotarians.

Home is not a thing of position, or standing.

My home is where the working people are, where you still see a Torino every now and then, and people still use motor oil to kill the mange.

It is where the men live who know how to fix their own damn water pump, where the women watch their soap operas on an ancient VCR because they will be at work at midday.

It is where the churches are small, and the houses, too. It is where people cheer for a college they have never seen, where propane tanks shine silver outside mobile homes with redwood decks, where buttercups burst up out of mounds of red mud, encircled by an old tire.

These are not the people of influence who have their names

carved into the concrete of banks and schools and churches, whose faces stare back from the society page. As I've said, maybe too many times, these are the descendants of people who could only get their name in the newspaper or the history books if they knocked some rich guy off his horse.

I do not, greatly, give a damn about writing about people who history will handle with great care, anyway, by birthright.

I will write about a one-armed man who used to sling a slingblade out by the county jail, and a pulpwood truck driver who could swing a pine pole around like a baseball bat.

I will write about dead police chiefs who treated even the most raggedy old boy with a little respect, and old men who sip beer beside the pool tables in Brother's Bar, and then go take some money off the college boys.

I will write about the wrongdoers, because sometimes doing right is just too damn hard, and the sorry drunks, and the women who love them anyway. I will write about mommas, not somebody's Big Daddy. I will write about snuff, not caviar.

I will write and write as long as somebody, anybody, wants me to, till we remind one more heartbroken ol' boy of his grandfather, or educate one more pampered Yankee on the people of the pines.

I will put on my necktie and do my best to fit in the more comfortable places, and it may be that I have come to like that too much. But it will never last for me, there, and I will always go back to what I understand and admire, and love.

And it may be that there will come a time when no one wants to know, when no amount of skill will make them want to know, or care. And then I will quit, and I will do something else, or just die, because all this jaw-jutting will wear out a man.

But the stories will last whether I do or not, count whether I do or not, and the rich folks will just have to get used to the idea that their stories are only part of the story, and not the only part worthy of the clay, and the pines, and the years.

Haunted Mansions

I Ain't Scared of You

As a boy, every October, I used to peek from beneath a hundred-year-old quilt and scare myself stupid with late-night monster movies that haunted the airwaves over our house. The antenna picked up only two channels—well, three, if you twisted it toward Red Mountain.

It remains my favorite time of year. The foothills blazed in reds and golds as the cool air nudged an endless summer. County fairs lit up the night in a whirl of neon, and porches glowed orange with pumpkins. Only the monsters on the Philco were in black and white. I still watch them every fall, all relics of the past, like me. Now I watch and smile.

I mean, what was I thinking?

The Mummy? Boris Karloff, who was swaddled in about three hundred miles of gauze, crept across the floor in a kind of inexorable stagger, dragging one foot. One arm, I believe, was bound to his side. The other, he waved stiffly as he moved toward his victims, as fast as a man in a full body cast could go.

"Run!" I would urge his victims, inside my seven-year-old mind. But now I know it was not necessary to even hurry. Just walk away, for heaven's sake. Or saunter, or stroll. Stop and have lunch. And when he catches up, moaning, walk a little bit farther. Do anything but stand there, screaming, while waiting . . . and waiting . . . to be done in. The thing is, the victims always seemed to be surprised.

Frankenstein? The monster in this movie was a plodder, created without joints. Also, he appeared unable to bend at the waist. How, then, would he get through the doorframe? He would just smack his head over and over again.

The Blob? It moved like Karo syrup. My granny could outrun a blob.

Creature from the Black Lagoon? Not as swift on dry land. But in the movies, people tend to be stupid. And when the victims-to-be did run from a monster, they always fell down. They did not trip on anything. They just fell.

Dracula? He scared me in 1966. Now I figure I could wait for him to turn into a bat and take him out with a Swiffer.

The Werewolf? Please. I have hairy kinfolk who howl at the moon and burst out of their pants.

The Invisible Man? He would never make it across the road here. Alabama drivers will run over you even when they do see you. The old movies that still frighten me are about creatures that grew to insane proportions, like giant ants and spiders and that one about the octopus that rose from the deep and threatened to eat, I believe, San Francisco. I thought I was over that one, too, but I ordered octopus at a Greek restaurant in Tarpon Springs, Florida, and it all came writhing back to me. Nothing, after being boiled, should still be jiggling.

I saw a movie recently about—no kidding—a giant snail. I'm not exactly a track star, but I think even I could outrun an escargot.

Free Spirits

❧

I NOTICED IT WHILE I WAS ON MY BOOK TOUR, traveling across the South . . . sometimes even in Wichita, Kansas. I
was in a different old hotel or historic-mansion-turned-bed-and-
breakfast every night because a man of my stature should not be
pried out of an Uber at an Airbnb. (I don't know what any of that
means, but it's what the cool kids are saying.) Nor should a man
of my age endure a dreaded "European-style" hotel, where one
must towel dry with a dishrag and know how to spell "shampoo"
in German.

Being a Southern writer, I usually stayed in a place with some
history, which (down here) means it's haunted. Every night, before
I could even get settled in properly, I had to deal with a ghost story.
This involved checking the closets, under the bed, and even down
the dark hallway. I never saw a specter, though I once almost died
of fright when I stumbled over a room service tray full of Buffalo
wing carcasses on my way to the ice machine—which is why, even
if it is right next door, it's always best to wear pants to make a trek
like that. But I digress.

Every Southern hotel, mansion, or plantation has a ghost, either
a creaking Confederate colonel wailing over his doomed ideals or
a gauzy young woman searching the halls for her lost cotillion.

There are apparitions in lighted windows and cold places in kitchens and (now this is the creepiest) little girls chasing balls down long hallways for eternity. The old Omni Grove Park Inn in Asheville, North Carolina, has one, but I wonder sometimes if it might have been an unhappy toddler being half-dragged to her room by a red-faced mother. Maybe, come to think of it, this is what being haunted really is: vacation with a two-year-old.

But my point is, why is it always rich folks' residences that are haunted? Does every person who is stinking wealthy in the Deep South get to have a ghost? I mean, when was the last time you walked into a place with a winding staircase that did not have an apparition posed atop it, some poor waif with a broken heart who flung herself from the battlements? Savannah alone has three hundred ghosts who are, at this moment, standing on a spiral staircase. Who ever heard of a haunted carport?

I guess it is just an entitlement or inheritance, like the family silver Aunt Minnie hid in the root cellar when she heard the Yankees a'comin'. If you're rich here, you get a ghost—that and a fox stole and sometimes a Buick.

We have spirits in the foothills of the Appalachians, in the working-class South, but by God, we have to earn them. If we want a ghost, we actually have to kill someone to get it; no one just gives it to us. My great-grandfather left us with one at a place called the Mill Branch in northeastern Alabama, but the less said about this, I suppose, the better. We still see it walking through the moonlight, though the number of confirmed sightings is in direct proportion to the number of beer bottles consumed. Funny how the spirit world is the only thing that alcohol brings into focus.

The Ghost of Halloweens Past

ONCE, BEFORE THE WONDER OF IMAGINATION began to petrify inside the husk of this old grouch that I have become, I viewed the coming of Halloween with an anticipation I could barely endure.

The question haunted us, at recess, on the big yellow bus, in the lunchroom at Roy Webb Elementary. A small army of cowlicks and hand-me-downs and Husky Boy jeans, we hunched over our sloppy joes, fish sticks, and chicken surprise and plotted our great transformation.

"What you gon' be?" they asked me.

"Not a ghost," I said.

I had gone trick-or-treating as a ghost the October before, waddling around the East Side and the mill village inside a big, threadbare pillowcase. But the grown-ups had been less than meticulous about spacing the eyeholes and I could see out of only one—the other was somewhere near my opposing ear. They had warned me to watch for cars, but mostly I just had to listen.

One year, I wrapped myself in toilet paper, head to toe. I meant to be Boris Karloff from *The Mummy*. But it rained, and I disintegrated, and looked less like a mummy than a very large, walking . . . well, you know.

But I'd learned the hard way that I had to come up with something. Once, when I was very small, I had shown up at my mean girl cousins' house without a costume, and they snatched me up and put makeup on me and dragged me along, dressed as a little doll . . . a girl doll. I'm still trying to recover from that.

Best to plan ahead.

I am sometimes inclined to whitewash the past, at least a little bit, but I do miss the simplicity of that time, and the effort and imagination we exhausted to be something or someone else for one night of the year. Our people were working people—mill workers and cotton pickers and pulpwooders and women who ran the machines in the sweatshops. We would join them in that life, probably. But for one night, we shaped a sword from a yardstick, fashioned an eye patch from quilt scrap, grabbed a single clip-on earring when no one was looking, and set off to search the Spanish Main for buried treasure . . . and Butterfinger bars.

I think it was better, in the end, than spending the biggest part of a hundred-dollar bill for a rubberized zombie costume that drips fake blood. There were no costume stores in Jacksonville, Alabama, in 1965, unless you count the dime store. There, if you managed to get your mother to crack the seal on her change purse, you had two choices: a witch or Daniel Boone.

No, it was better to plot, to plan, to imagine, to take something from a book you read, a story you heard. Our mothers could sew. We could dream. It is amazing how far you could get with that, even as a one-eyed Casper, a plastic pumpkin bumping against your leg, or a wet and ragged mummy, melting into the night.

Praise the Gourd

HALLOWEEN USED TO BE SIMPLE. You got a punkin', cut off the top of its head, gouged out its stringy orange insides, and carved a face on it that looked like your brother. But that just wasn't good enough for some folks.

I realize this may mark me as one of those people who resurface every October, hollering about the perils of Halloween. Not me. I have been quietly celebrating it a long time and have never been moved, no matter how many bushels of candy corn I consumed, to run off and worship the Devil. But I fear this holiday has lost its soul.

I blame the zombies.

Don't pretend you haven't noticed, what with all their moaning and lurching and . . . well, I guess moan and lurch is all they do, if you don't count standing around looking walleyed and gnashing their bad teeth. You can't swing a dead black cat this time of year without knocking a few down like bowling pins, which is not hard to do, considering they move at the pace of a box turtle, more nuisance than fright. Anything I can walk briskly away from—and that list gets shorter every year—is unlikely to strike fear in my heart. I figure I should still be able to out-sprint a zombie when I am 115. That is, if they don't annoy me to death first.

I should not care so deeply about them, but there are so many rubber-legging around these days that they threaten to become the iconic image of my favorite time of year. Halloween has always been, to me, a time to smile at things that frighten us, to watch the night sky for witches but encounter them only as they walk down the street on the way to Ruby Tuesday. I used to be afraid of vampires, but how can you fear one three feet tall, squinting in my porch light, trying not to swallow their drug-store fangs when their mommas smack them upside the head for forgetting to say "thank you" for the Sugar Babies.

Mostly I love Halloween because it is the orange-and-black beginning of a season that tumbles into Thanksgiving, which tumbles into Christmas. And zombies just seem a little out of place in that. Thanksgiving should have nothing to do with armies of shuffling undead. Don't get me started on Christmas. The only undead at Christmas should be Jacob Marley, wailing about greed.

The iconic image of Halloween should be the pun'kin. The pun'kin, carved into faces that are scary only because we want them to be, winking from every front porch. The pun'kin, cast in plastic, swinging from the hands of knee-high princesses, leering back from department store shelves, until it gives way to tins of butter cookies.

But I fear for the pun'kin. How long before he is kicked down the street by zombie hordes, booted into obscurity? Young people tell me that no one—no one—wants to dress up like a pun'kin anymore. All a pun'kin does, they say, is sit there, and glow.

This may be true, all of it, but try to make a pie out of a zombie, and see where that gets you. Though I hear that, when it comes to pies, your canned zombie is the way to go.

A Homespun Ghost Story

⁓

GHOSTS PEERED DOWN FROM THE RAFTERS, people said. When the old mill finally shut down, after shaking the earth of my hometown for a hundred years, workers who stayed on to dismantle its machines said they heard strange things when they walked the vast, echoing rooms. They heard footsteps and an unsettling, whispering sound, as if generations who had worked themselves to death refused to depart just because the rich men closed the doors. The place had always been haunted, old people said. Spirits swirled in the air white with cotton dust, and the machines seemed hungry. Some say the mansions are haunted down here, but if ghosts linger anywhere, I believe, it is behind the padlocked gates of the redbrick monoliths you find, crumbling, in many Southern towns. I know it is foolishness, but sometimes I ride past the place our mill stood and think of her, and wonder if she haunts this place, and if she looks over her people, still.

My friend Homer Barnwell told me about the old woman and promised to tell me more, but he walks with the angels now. I often think of her in this season of the black cat, the glowing pumpkin smile, and boys who shout "boo" from under bedsheets, and sometimes I wish I knew more, but usually I don't. The point of Halloween is to know enough to scare you a little; and never look under the sheet.

A child of mill workers here in Jacksonville, Alabama, Homer told me of a woman tall as a man in old-fashioned hook-and-eye shoes, with silver hair that hung to the hem of her black dress.

Her face was like cut pine, and her eyes were like honey. They say she had Indian blood; that's where she learned her remedies, and charms. She came, like everyone in the village, from the mountains, among the starved-out hillbillies who took their stations at the machines.

Homer was a boy the first time he saw her, on a street paved in soot and cinders, and his mother warned him not to stare. She would turn a rude boy into a doodlebug, or at least that was what the little boys lied about when they were getting dog sick on rabbit tobacco behind the cotton shed. But as he got older, he saw the truth of it: In a place where the company owned the doctor, being sick meant being fired, and the old woman made medicines for men with brown lung and picked herbs to help women with morning sickness, so they could keep their places at the machines. She protected them the best she could from the Yankee outsiders who had no respect for them or the magic of the mountains.

The mill owner was not good to his people. He paid them near nothing and did not weep when the machines wrecked their bodies. He starved them to break a strike in 1933 and watched them suffer from his great house. The old woman watched, too, with her amber eyes.

In time, the rich man began to wither and fail, and his great house rotted around him, and all fell to death and ruin. The people worked on. And some said she aided in this, somehow, but of course it was just the passing of time.

Just foolishness of course, just a story to tell, on a night when the bedsheet beasties walk the earth.

Christmas in a Can

Planes, Trains, and Turkeys

I CANNOT REMEMBER exactly where I had been that November, just that I was trying to get home. I remember I was still a young man then, connecting in Atlanta—me and everyone else—most of us trying to get home to a turkey dinner that seemed like the most important thing in the world. The home we were bound for, most of us, was not the one on our water bill, where we made our living and our beds, but the original home, where our people are, and time was running out. If such a gathering of strangers can wear a single, shared expression, we did, wrapped in worry.

The delays piled up, the clock ticked, and babies cried.

I did not miss a Thanksgiving in my first twenty-one years. Then, my editor sent me on my first plane ride to cover the Texas vs. Texas A&M game in College Station.

"What about Thanksgiving?" I had wondered.

But I went and did my duty. I drove a rented Fairmont to a packed stadium, where well-meaning people in the press box served turkey, mashed potatoes, and green peas that had an otherworldly, greenish glow. At home, a ham bone simmered in pinto beans, a million miles from me. I remember that Texas won, and as I drove to the hotel in thick fog, I made a wrong turn and—I am not making this up—somehow wound up trapped inside an escaped herd of bovines.

Somewhere, my mother was putting leftover biscuits in a tub and pecan pie in aluminum foil, but all I could think was: What if they stampede?

The second time it happened, I was marooned in Los Angeles. I clawed together the last of my quarters and got a small ham, and called my momma and asked her how to make pinto beans, but when it was done it tasted like scorched lunch meat plopped in a mud puddle.

I remember I went to the ocean in search of solace, which is what Californians do. But solace plumb evaded me. I did learn two things, on the dirty sand: One, you cannot replicate home in a shiny, never-used pot from Ralphs supermarket; and two, pretty as it is, the Pacific is like ice water for a Southern boy.

I missed another one, in Tampa Bay; I think it had to do with the transmission on a '66 Mustang. I missed another in Palm Beach, the year we failed to elect a president democratically because of something called a hanging chad. I ate at IHOP, feeling sorry for myself over the Rooty Tooty Fresh 'N Fruity, and swore I would never, ever miss Thanksgiving again.

In the airport, we waited, and waited. But as I watched people fret, sticky from Cinnabons, I noticed a harried-looking young mother coo to her toddler about all the good things they would eat, the people he would see, for the first time. People talked recipes, and spoke of kin, both beloved and sorry. "Do you think he will be there . . . ?" And, in my eavesdropping, I discovered a rare peace of mind.

The fact is, all I was rushing home to rediscover was not lost because the planes did not fly.

It unfolded, warmly, deliciously, timelessly, just out of reach, and it really is enough to know a thing endures, lives on, just beyond your touch, your presence. You can live inside that, knowing that it does.

I hope this makes sense, somehow, and I hope you all make it home.

Socks, Underwear, and a Camaro

～つ

D EAR SANTA (or whoever),
Apparently, you did not get my letter this time last year. I understand how this can happen.

Mail must be unpredictable up there, in the permafrost. It may be that a reindeer ate it. It could happen. We have a donkey down here in Alabama that ate the cuff off my sport coat. Really. But I digress.

I know you did not get my letter because I did not receive the Camaro (pearl white, convertible, V-8, with saddle-tan interior) I hinted so strongly for you to bring me on Christmas morning. I am not bitter about it. I will just keep rattling around in the same old smoking, raggedy, twelve-year-old Toyota, till it wheezes to a shuddering stop, probably in front of the scrapyard.

If it should break down, in traffic, while I am taking my poor old mother to the doctor, I suppose that is not your fault. Do not worry about us. We will probably be fine. I am sure someone would pull over, if they saw us limping, me and my eighty-year-old mother, through the ragweed along the side of the interstate. Anyway, someone probably needed that Camaro a lot worse than we did, probably some spoiled teenager who stopped believing in you when she was five.

It is a little harder, down here, to believe, because the very idea of a sled is hard to imagine in red mud or soybeans or saw palmetto. Yet I still do, though I admit my conviction is becoming a little strained.

I mean, I did not ask for an Italian sports car. I did not even write to you for a new Land Cruiser. I hinted for a Chevy. But I guess that doesn't matter, since you never saw my note.

This made me suspicious, though: While I did not get the convertible I hinted at, I did get the underwear and socks. That makes me think I might have been right in my supposition that you do not even see most of the letters sent to you at the North Pole, and that you have some poor flunky screen your mail. That must be why everybody gets socks and underwear.

It may even be, considering the volume of correspondence you must receive, that you have outsourced the work to some offshore clearing center, or, worse, have it handled digitally. This brings tears to my eyes, though I guess there is no reason why you would be any different from any other private corporation or public utility. Not long ago, for instance, I called 411 on my Verizon to get the number for a barbecue restaurant and got three lawyers and a toe doctor. Even though I knew it was a computer, I cussed it sideways. But I digress, again.

Santa, or whatever overworked elf is actually reading this, I have decided to give you a second chance. It is said that you have magical powers, and I have seen in movies that you can read the mind of a child who writes you and thinks only of others, asks only for them, and you bring him a choo choo anyway.

So I ask, once more, only for good things for people close to me, and maybe good things for the whole wide world.

And snow. I would like to see some snow. Falling on a Ferrari. If I ain't gonna get a Camaro, I might as well not get a Ferrari.

The Canned Stuff

~⌒

IT JUST WASN'T Thanksgiving till the shaking commenced.

My mother's turkey would already be out of the oven and resting on the stove top, still steaming in a lake of butter and seasonings, the ancient, blackened roasting pan wedged in right next to a big pan of my Aunt Jo's cornbread dressing. The biscuits were done, along with the mashed potatoes, sweet potatoes, pinto beans and ham, creamed onions, and all the rest. The pound cakes and pecan pies waited on the sideboard.

But there could be no feast, not even grace, until I saw my sainted mother shaking in the kitchen like she had grabbed a naked wire. The first time I witnessed it, as a little boy, I thought perhaps she might be possessed or going into convulsions.

"No," she said. "I'm just tryin' to get this cranberry sauce out of this can."

She would twist off the lid with her hand-cranked can opener—she did not trust the electric kind, which sounded faintly demonic, like a rock-and-roll record played backward—and aim the can at a clean plate. Then she went to town.

She shook straight up and down, mostly, but sometimes she had to go a little sideways, until finally it slid out in one neat, cylindrical shape and plopped down on the plate.

Thank you, Lord, we all thought, and the prayer had not even begun yet. She sliced it into neat circles, each a half-inch thick.

"John," she said to my uncle, "will you say the blessin'?"

I didn't know cranberries or jellied cranberries or whatever you call them came any other way. I guess I was in junior high school before I ever even knew it started with an actual fruit. Most of you will probably roll your eyes at this, despite knowing good and well that your momma was shaking all over your kitchen, too.

When I was of dating age, I sat down to more formal Thanksgiving dinners and saw my first real cranberry, in what I think they called a "chutney." I believe this was also the first time I ever witnessed a turkey with those little booties at the end of its drumsticks. And I thought this was kind of mean, to tart up the poor thing after it was already dead and gone.

But anyway, I digress. I can't say I didn't like the rich folks' version of cranberry sauce, but it wasn't the same.

A lifetime later, I was stranded in West Palm Beach, Florida, on a Thanksgiving Day, feeling sorry for myself. I ate dinner at a Denny's or an IHOP or something like it. It was either eat that or order some mu shu pork from across the street or grab a Little Debbie cake and a pint of milk.

The waiter brought out the turkey and dressing with a little sliver of cranberry sauce, just like Momma would shake loose. Somebody back in that kitchen had to shake it, too, to get it there. And for some reason, I did not feel so very far away from home.

Not long ago, I wrote a book about Jerry Lee Lewis, perhaps the most famous shaker of all time. I heard him play "Whole Lotta Shakin' Goin' On" in New York City, and he dedicated it to me.

The crowd went wild. I got hungry.

Dear Santa (Again)

~⌒

DEAR SANTA,
   (If this letter is read by an assistant, flunky, or go-between, please be so kind as to forward it immediately to the jolly old elf himself, and do not tell me he has to bring joy to children all over the world and his time is valuable. I got three jobs. He rides in a sleigh and checks a list.

(Checking it twice does not count as two jobs. I still have one more job than him. As for that sleigh ride, it's a sleigh ride, in the air. I rode in back of a Lincoln Continental once all the way to Oxford, Mississippi. I did not consider it work.)

Anyway, I'll get right to it. Most of my friends tell me I am too old to believe in you, let alone write you a letter, but since I have ceased to believe in you, I have discovered that mostly what I get for Christmas is shaving products, underwear, purple velour pullovers, and soap-on-a-rope.

I have decided I believe in you again.

So here's my list. You do not need to worry yourself about whether I have been naughty or nice. I have been nice. Trust me. Ask my mom. Do not just ask around, indiscriminately, as this is not professional behavior. You know what? Don't even ask Mom, who can hold a grudge. I stayed out all night when I was seventeen and she still throws it up to me, like hanging out in the parking lot at Hardee's was a bacchanalia.

Anyway, in keeping with the spirit of the season, I am unselfishly asking mostly for things for other people, though if you would like to throw in a convertible Camaro, pearl white, with saddle-tan leather interior, I would believe in you a real, real whole lot.

No?

Well, I took a shot.

For my big brother, Sam, I would like you to send a cinder block. He can place it atop his foot, when he drives. I once wrote that all he needed to pass for an old woman behind the wheel was a pillbox hat and pearls, but have since decided that is insulting . . . to old women. Old women blow right past him.

For my mother, I would like a magic dust that changes cats into reindeer. Then, I will sell all thirteen of them to you cheap. Donner and Blitzen must be dragging a little bit by now, since they are about 142 years old. If that is unreasonable, I would like a carload of Tender Vittles. Them things are breaking me. Also for my mother, I would like a convertible Camaro, white, with saddle-tan interior. We will only use it to haul cat food and take her to the toe doctor. I promise.

(Please also send one to my aunts. I wore out their cars when I was sixteen, just going to buy hamburgers. Santa, it is the right thing to do.)

Oh, and how about some peace on earth. That is sometimes a little strained down here, when my kinfolks get all hopped up on eggnog and Little Debbies.

I do not think any of this is unreasonable. For myself, again, I ask nothing. My life is imperfect, littered, but still better than I deserve. I can always use socks.

I Beg Your Pardon

DEAR MR. PRESIDENT,

I am sorry for bothering you in this hectic season, and I hate to take you away from the eighteenth hole and your negotiations with the prince of something or other.

I'm a man who believes in traditions; we are funny that way down here. One of my favorites is the annual holiday photo opportunity at the White House involving the president, his family, and the presidential turkey.

He—or she?—is always a really fine specimen of poultry and is still very much alive there on what I believe is the White House lawn. I do not know how they get the turkey to stand still long enough for a photo, since turkeys are not known for their attention spans. I think they used to bring the gobbler into the residence itself, but being a country boy, I can tell you that is not a good idea. But I digress. . . .

I used to think it was sad that the bird would, as soon as the paparazzi were gone, be led into the White House kitchen and then be, well, dispatched. I know this makes me a hypocrite, since I have helped send many turkeys to their dooms without a care.

But I did not know them. They were not THE American turkey. The ones that I consumed came from the Piggly Wiggly; they were hard frozen and wrapped in plastic. As a little boy, watching that great turkey pose for the networks, I darn near cried.

Then, year after year, the camera would turn to the smiling reporters who explained that the turkey had just been pardoned and would be retired to a pleasant farm in the country to live out its days. And I was so happy.

This Thanksgiving, though, I have some concerns. I know that you can tend to be, well, a little pugnacious. You ran on a promise to do away with politics as usual in Washington. Well, the presidential turkey usually gets a pardon.

While I know you have a reputation to uphold and might think that if you pardon the bird, it will appear as if you're soft on crime, I do not believe this is the case.

I think you'll appear presidential and benevolent—but, you know, not in any sissy kind of way. If it will make you feel better, you can chastise the turkey vigorously first, perhaps on Twitter. The thing is, Mr. President, that turkey deserves to live.

This year, I recommend ordering out for your Thanksgiving spread. Maybe on your way down to Florida, you could wheel through Alabama and get a whole dinner to go at Bates House of Turkey Restaurant in Greenville. Every day is Thanksgiving there.

Please at least think about my request to be lenient, and remember, Christmas is coming.

The Christmas Kid

～

THEY SAY CHRISTMAS IS FOR CHILDREN. It sounds pretty to say it.

Me, I am not so sure. My big brother, Sam, is in his dotage, and I am fairly certain Christmas is for him.

The very young wait and fret, almost twitching, for a single, glittering moment. They tear feverishly into a package it took their grandmother an hour to adorn. They watch their parents untangle miles of lights, gasp and coo when the bulbs blink on, and then are bored stupid within three minutes and go back to playing on their phones. They gnaw the head off a chocolate Rudolph, devour seven sugar-sprinkled cookies and the roof off a gingerbread house, and then begin to jerk and vibrate in such a glucose overdose it's a wonder they don't strap on their *Guardians of the Galaxy* rocket boots and shoot for the moon.

Christmas is wasted on such as them. But the old . . . the miracle for them is in remembering a lifetime of Christmases past in every new season. Which, I guess, means the season is for children, after all.

I love this time—every mile of country road and every aisle in every store picks the lock on one of those memories. I see a single strand of new age, fiber-optic Christmas lights and think about the old, fat, faulty lights that surrounded our cedar tree, usually stolen from the state right-of-way. There were always a half dozen of those lights—the blown ones—in a bowl on a coffee table, like a garnish. I remember how the hot bulbs would cause the tinsel—which I think might have been made from old aluminum siding—to wrinkle and thin, and even as a little boy, I'd think: Well, that ain't good.

Every turkey in every Piggly Wiggly made me think of Charles Dickens. Once, in Winn-Dixie, I saw a goose. I almost danced for joy. Even now, I can smell chocolate-covered cherries across a drugstore. I see tangerines and Brazil nuts and almost cry. I even like the television commercials; it ain't Christmas till you see Santa Claus riding a Philips Norelco shaver.

Yet, compared to my older brother, I am the Grinch himself. He is, most of the year, a terrible grouch. It's a lifetime condition that has worsened in old age. When I was small, I waited patiently—waited years—till he finally got hung up in a barbed wire fence, to bust him with a rock. I thought it would somehow improve him. I would not do it again, but someone needs to. It might take this time.

But at Christmas, his spirit rises. The weather and the years have left their mark on him, but in this season, I see the boy who knocked mistletoe from the high branches with his pellet rifle and waited up all night listening for Santa Claus and then shook me awake with excitement on his face, in his voice. He always woke me and never left me behind. He always said the same thing.

"He's done come."

"Did you see him?" I would ask.

"Nawwwww," he'd say. "Nobody does."

Even now, in his sixties, he loves this time. He and my sister-in-law, Teresa, light up their house with twinkling lights. A plastic Santa Claus, a relic from our childhood, shines on season after season on the porch. "Sam's a kid 'bout Christmas," she says. How wonderful, for that to be absolutely true.

Bah, Humbug!

⁓

THE BOOK WAS NOT TREATED WELL. The fabric on the back cover seems to have been eaten away by some dreaded pestilence, probably one long-ago summer. This book was not made for summer, I suppose. At some point, it was left out in the rain. The ink has run, but I can still make out the words. It has an odd beginning, for a book about joy.

> Marley was dead: to begin with. There is no doubt whatever about that . . . dead as a doornail . . . I might have been inclined, myself, to regard a coffin-nail as the deadest piece of ironmongery in the . . .

You, no doubt, have traditions you return to every Christmas. This is mine. I bought it for three dollars at a thrift store, but it was the best three dollars I ever spent. In *A Christmas Carol,* I've found a time machine in which I can move, not just across decades and even oceans but spirit. It makes me feel good. It makes me hopeful in an age when it sometimes seems like we've lost our hearts.

I am not saying it transforms me, as the spirits of Christmases past, present, and yet to come do to miserly Ebenezer Scrooge. But in a way that's hard to put into words, I find wisdom in it, and in the confusing whirl of my twenty-first-century life, a little peace . . . maybe even cheer.

The truest lines might be those of Jacob Marley's first ghostly manifestation in Scrooge's bedchamber, as he wafts in dragging a great chain of lockboxes and timepieces.

"You are fettered," said Scrooge, trembling. "Tell me why?"

"I wear the chain I forged in life," replied the Ghost. "I made it link by link, and yard by yard; I girded it on of my own free-will, and of my own free-will I wore it. Is its pattern strange to you?"

I swear, some days, I hear a faint clinking myself.

"At this time of the rolling year," the spectre said, "I suffer most. Why did I walk through crowds of fellow-beings with my eyes turned down, and never raise them to that blessed Star which led the Wise Men to a poor abode! Were there no poor homes to which its light would have conducted me!"

I've tried to be generous, but there is more to this book than that. It is, of course, a warning not to waste your years, as Marley did, but to discover that cheer that sent old Fezziwig cavorting about the dance floor.

Well, I don't dance. But there are many things about this time of year that just lift me, somehow, that make my tread less heavy, even if the closest I get to a Christmas tree is seeing one in a commercial on a hotel television.

I don't go to many parties and have missed a lifetime of Christmas services. I hear the bells toll, usually from a distance. But even in this solitude, Dickens—and Scrooge—found joy.

"His own heart laughed: and that was quite enough for him."

Better Watch Out

~⌒

D EAR RICK,
       I don't usually answer mail around Christmas. I am busy
in December, and—let me tell you—these elves can be a handful
when they're all hopped-up on fruitcake and divinity candy. Last
week, they got into some sugarplums, and Mrs. Claus had to peel
'em off the walls. Now the post office at the North Pole is hopelessly backed up. It's all "gimme, gimme, gimme" this time of year,
and you've got no idea how hard it is to load a sleigh with 1,678,543
puppies (not one of them potty-trained). But I digress.

    I am writing you for two reasons. One, I rarely get letters from
people who are almost old enough for Social Security. Two, you
persist, year after year, in ticking me off. You imply every Yuletide
that you've been good and deserve some special present, usually
a Camaro. Who do you think you are talking to? I am Santa Claus,
for Pete's sake.

> He sees you when you're sleeping
> He knows when you're awake
> He knows if you've been bad or good . . .

Remember that part right there. I know everything. You think
I wasn't listening when you cussed out that referee during the

Alabama-Clemson game . . . come to think of it, in all of the Alabama-Clemson games? The last time I heard that kind of language was at an insurance salesmen's convention in Las Vegas in 1963. And I still remember what you hid under your mattress in 1974, 1975, 1976—well, let's just say the seventies were a disappointing period. I should have left you coal and switches for the entire decade, maybe even through the Reagan administration—both terms.

This year alone, you said 87,853 bad words, and that was just while driving through Atlanta. And don't think that I have not been keeping up with your career, if you can call it that. All you've done for about twenty-five years is write a few books, and when you sign them, your penmanship looks like that of a drunken monkey. Tighten up.

You don't even seem to be improving. Most people get a little better in old age, if for no other reason than they just get tired, but not you. You manage to do bad things with almost no effort, like a man who lies in bed holding a BB gun, shooting holes in the walls. Wait, that was you, too, back in 1969, when you had your leg in a cast. Good grief!

Still, you insist on asking me for high-end items, things I would not bring you even if you had been good. Have you given thought in your selfish mind to the logistics of it all, to how hard it is to fit a sports car into a sack? I dang near killed Blitzen last year dragging all those automobiles around the sky. Donner still talks about me behind my back. Rick, maybe it's time you thought of someone besides yourself and tried to do just a tiny bit better. I'll be watching, terrified to blink.

With best wishes for the season,
Santa
P.S. I hope you like the socks.

A Hard Bargain

I HAVE BEEN SCARED OF A FEW THINGS in my life, but, across the years, I've tried to cowboy up and get over them. I used to be afraid of heights; even a barn loft or the roof of a Winnebago made me dizzy. So I hitched myself to a rope and rappelled down a rock face on Chandler Mountain from so high you could look down and see the hawks circling. I don't think I screamed once, except maybe inside my own head. I used to be afraid of copperheads, till I watched an old woman go to town on one with a hoe handle and then go make me some tea cakes. I am not a squeamish man, mostly. The only thing that terrifies me still is what they call, ominously, Black Friday.

It sounds like something from the Dark Ages, from the plague years. I've never actually experienced one, but I've heard the awful stories.

One minute, you're saying grace around a Thanksgiving turkey, grateful for all the good things in your life—like hot biscuits, cornbread dressing, candied sweet potatoes, and (oh, yeah) friends and family. Full, tired, and happy, you slip into a soft chair and, surrounded by the people you love, vanish into a deep sleep.

The next minute, you're tugging on one end of a flat-screen TV, trying to wrest it from the grip of a rabid grandmother who, teeth bared, is calling you names that should never be uttered on the cusp of the Yuletide.

Or so I am told.

The truth is, I've been too afraid to see it all for myself, even if you can buy a refrigerator for seventeen dollars with a clip-out coupon. For days, the mailbox has been crammed with circulars that promise seasonal savings on everything from pickup trucks to printer ink to pistachios, and I think that a real man would just gird his loins, sharpen his American Express card, and do battle. But then I imagine the shoppers—faces all aglow, clashing through the toy department and all the way out to their minivans, each with half a teddy bear held aloft in grim triumph—and I lose my nerve. I find myself a sturdy chair and a stack of catalogs and shop from the safety and comfort of home, even if I do have to pay full price and a ten-thousand-dollar delivery fee, even though L.L.Bean is almost always plumb out of size XXL double long.

I'm told that there is a far safer method, something called the Internet, but I hear they can be a rough bunch, too. So I'll stick to the catalogs. I think the operator at The Vermont Country Store genuinely likes me. Now and then, my kinfolks, who are braver and tougher, shame me. They get me a present they fought for, suffered for, in the melee and misery of a Black Friday, and I think that, next Christmas, I will be brave.

So watch out, Grandma. I'm coming for you and that bargain flat-screen, and you'd better not get in the way of my Christmas shopping, if you know what's good for you.

Can I Get an Amen?

⁓

So, Rick," the host said, "what are you thankful for?"

"Good friends," I said. I always say that. I draw it like a gun.

We don't do this at my house, where the pre-Thanksgiving-dinner prayer, an opus in itself, takes a pretty good while, so we don't have time for foolishness. I believe that, if we made my kin-folks wait any longer to dig into my mother's roast turkey, one or more of us might fall to the floor and begin to twitch.

But I have been to other people's houses where, as part of their tradition, they go around the table, before the meal, and ask each person to tell a little story about something for which they are, in that critical moment, with dinner laid out and steaming on the table, thankful.

This would not be a heartwarming exercise in my house. People tortured by a lifetime of Congregational Holiness blessings would not hem and haw, searching for the sweetest thing to say. They would, if nothing came to mind fairly soon, make something up. "I am thankful for trees." "I, too, am thankful for trees." "Me, too." And so on, around the table.

But some people cannot think on their feet. They balk and stammer and fret so long that I have, in all honesty, wanted to jab them with my fork and snap small children with a rubber band.

They stare off into space and get lost there, for long minutes, while the butter slowly congeals on the mashed potatoes and the rolls go as cold as the Pillsbury whop 'em can from whence they sprang.

I have—and I'm not proud of this—actually tried to exercise some form of telepathy, some sort of mind control to nudge a bewildered person toward an answer, before the french-fried onions on the green bean casserole sogged into an unspeakable mess.

Say anything, I willed.

Say, I willed, world peace, or cats. Maybe not cats.

But I do not possess this gift. The turkey just sits there, cooling and forlorn, its little plump drumsticks with those little paper footies on the ends sticking in the air, all dressed up and nowhere to go.

I am fifty-seven. I do not have time—or a Thanksgiving—to waste. I will stay at home from here on out, till my last one has faded, sleepily, into football on television, and plans for Christmas, and the unmistakable rip and rustle of the aluminum foil my mother will use to cover the leftovers that are never left over for long.

My mother had a hard year—battled sickness and outlasted it. As we enter this holiday season, she will again be at the center of it as the keeper of its traditions and, in many ways, its joy.

We are a funny people, in a way, mountain people, and we do not always say to each other's faces what we appreciate, and what we cannot even imagine being without. It may be we think it is bad luck, somehow, or a weakness of sorts. I don't know. But we know our own hearts.

If we went around the table, to speak it out loud, somebody would probably say trees. But at least we could eat.

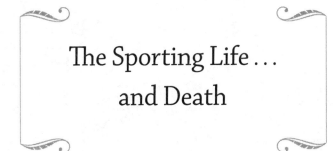

The Sporting Life . . .
and Death

Burying the Bear

॰॰॰

Y OU CAN'T LIVE DOWN HERE and not love that sound, that solid *thud* of a leather shoe making contact with a leather ball, and the roar that it brings. It may come from a field surrounded by rickety bleachers at a forlorn crossroads that is dark any other night except Friday or from a great stadium straining with a hundred thousand souls. It is yet a roar, and on that lovely sound, we'll ride from the misery of late summer to the dull wet of winter. In the meantime, life is just better, richer.

Hot dogs become delicacies. Parking lots become places of celebration, if not worship. Even the air is finer just because a kid encircled by a battered tuba warbles by.

When I hear these things, my heart lifts inside my chest and then breaks, just a little bit. I always think of the Bear—and enchiladas—and it almost makes me cry.

I was a young man when it happened, when the great Paul William "Bear" Bryant coached his last football game in a frigid Liberty Bowl in Memphis and then, before another season could begin without him, died, on January 26, 1983. He had passed into history and mythology long before, but his death sent newsrooms here in Alabama into a kind of frenzy. I, one of the very best newspapermen that you could hire in this world for minimum wage,

163

was dispatched to Birmingham, to interview the man who dug his grave.

Along with me was one of the most remarkable photographers ever to live, the great Ken Elkins, who looked a whole lot like Mark Twain. My 1976 Pontiac Grand Prix was running hot, so we left the premises of *The Anniston Star* in Ken's pickup, which might have been a Chevy or a Ford but was already old by the Korean War.

We had no plan, other than to ambush the gravedigger somewhere on the cemetery grounds, even if I had to throw Ken in front of his backhoe. We'd made it to Irondale, just this side of Birmingham, when the truck's transmission began to smoke and whine and we limped into a garage that promised absolutely nothing.

There was a Mexican restaurant across the street, and you could smell the tortilla chips frying. So we decided that was a better way to spend our downtime than standing in a cold parking lot wringing our hands. I might have had a margarita, to ward off the chill. I might have had a couple more. And on at least one of them, I toasted the greatest football coach of his time. It seems like, after the truck was fixed, we made a halfhearted stab at finding that gravedigger. Or maybe we didn't; my mind was not clear. I seem to remember Ken trying to shift gears while eating chips and salsa, all balanced on the steering wheel—or maybe that was just what Jose Cuervo wanted me to believe.

I have written before that I am not sorry we didn't get that interview, that I would not have wanted to look down on the grave. It's much better to remember the Bear growling along a sideline. He's the first thing I think of when the sounds, smells, and magic of this season descend—that, and pico de gallo.

Everybody has a Bear Bryant story here in Alabama. The one thing I am certain of is that every one of theirs is better than mine.

The Sweetest Sound

I CANNOT REMEMBER EVERYTHING but I remember that stingy moon, remember a sliver of cold in a black sky, thin and useless. You might as well try to light your way with a piece of broken glass, for all the good it was. My flashlight, a relic from the Korean War, had died about eighteen seconds after full dark. The boys in front of me, friends, brothers and cousins, mostly, were barely better off. They had to shake their hand-me-down batteries every few steps to coerce a last feeble glint of electricity, but I could have shaken mine like a Birmingham Hoochie Coo and still been walking in the dark. Only my brother Sam, who was born grown, who already had sideburns at age thirteen, had a good battery in his light. He was irritating that way. People said the day he was born he just dusted himself off in the hospital and walked home.

But, except for the threat of falling to our deaths down some crevasse, I guess we did not really need light. Our direction was determined not by what we could see but by what we could hear. We followed the sound across that frozen ground, followed a thing faint, constant, lovely, as we trudged single file across the haunted ridges and deep into the black hollows, the mist shining silver where that one good flashlight bored through the dark.

I can still hear it, after all these years. The poet in me—well, the never-was poet in me—would like to call it music, but it was prettier than that, prettier than I can say. It would have been nice to sit on a porch and hear it, but the other boys looked at me funny when I suggested that. Only the boys afraid of the dark, or of the cold, or of monsters, stayed home. I went, this one time, to show I was not one of them.

I was the youngest, and so the last in line. As we made our way diagonally up a ridge, rocks turning our ankles beneath the slick carpet of leaves, I felt myself begin to slide sickeningly straight down the mountain, straight toward what I knew to be a bone-breaking deadfall. I caught myself on a gummy pine sapling, breathed a minute, and started up again, even farther behind. No one had even turned around, and the romantic in me, the one that read about lost souls on desert islands, wondered how long I would have lain there, broken and forgotten. My brothers said I thought like that because I read too many books.

But falling was not romantic on the mountain. Falling was what you did up here. You walked; you fell. You chewed some Brown's Mule, or some Beech-Nut, if your stomach could handle it. I did not chew, so mostly I just walked and fell.

What a dumbass I was, I thought, as I slid again and lost thirty yards of the uphill ground I had gained. A smart boy would have chased some brighter light, somewhere, because the light was where the girls lived. A smart boy would have been in town, leaning on the hood of a car at the Rocket Drive-In with a cherry Coke in one hand and a beautiful woman in the other. Or, at least, that was how I figured it should be. I was not yet ten years old, and a beautiful woman would have sent me into a convulsion.

No, we went the *other* way, away from perfume and soft shoulders, gouging deeper and deeper into the dark, into the foothills of the Appalachians along the Alabama-Georgia line. It was November, maybe even as late as December, 1969, but it could have been any night, when boredom was stronger than common sense, after the cold sent the snakes down into the earth, and walking out into nothing was as much adventure as we could divine.

My big brother, Sam, was only three years older than me, but he drove a Willys Jeep he hacked out of a rust pile and made to live again by soaking its bones in buckets of dirty gasoline. And so, he got to walk in front. He had an ax in a tow sack, but no gun. This was as far from a gentleman's hunt as I guess a fellow could get.

We were all the same, us boys, on the outside. We did not own big parkas or camouflage anything, because while we still had real winter back then, it was too short in which to invest much wealth. We wore flannel shirts and thermal undershirts and something called a car coat, a thin and useless thing, which, as near as I could tell, was made out of polyester, cat hair, and itch. Walmart would, one day, sell a trillion of them. We got a new one every other year; that, and a gross of underwear.

The smart ones in the group wore two pairs of pants, even three, because the briars ripped at our legs with every step. Sometime, back in the times of our grandfathers, these mountains had been old-growth hardwoods and towering pines, but none of us could remember a time when the South looked like that. Old men talked of an age when the great trees towered into the clouds and the forest floor was dark and smooth and clean, but these mountains had been clear-cut generations before, creating a tangled mess of skinny trees fighting for the light, with undergrowth and saw briars strung between them like razor wire.

It was a time before hunting was a fashion. We hunted in our work boots, laced up around two pairs of socks—three, if you were growing into them. The ones who had gloves wore them and the ones who didn't walked through the woods with a pair of tube socks over our hands. I guess an outsider would have laughed at us, but outsiders did not get to go.

So armored, spitting and breathing hard, we attacked the mountain. And no one said a word. I tried to whine, once, and ducked just in time to avoid being slapped back down the mountain.

"Hush," my brother hissed, then, gentler: "Listen."

The baying was so thin it vanished in the wind in the trees.

But he could hear it plain.

"Joe," he said.

We often got things, back then, no one else wanted. We were the poorest relations, and naturally became the depository for things cracked, busted, rusted, or slightly burned. Kinfolks and other well-meaning people brought us these things with a straight face, but we knew. The dump charged between three and five dollars a load, while we took their castoffs for free, took their refrigerators that did not cool, and fans that did not spin, and big, heavy televisions stuck permanently on a horizontal roll. "You can fix it," they always said, and drove away. At one point, my Grandmother Ava had three radios on her dresser that were mute as a stone. People even brought us tires worn completely through. "You can get them recapped," they said. Now, how in the hell do you do that, unless your last name is Goodyear?

That is how we got Joe.

Joe was a coon dog, a fierce mixed-breed dog, a mass of quivering muscle and intelligence. You could see the black and tan in him, and bluetick, and even some red feist, but mostly he seemed comprised of thin white lines where his body had been ripped and torn, as if instead of breeding those bloodlines into him some Doctor Frankenstein had just sewed him together from spare parts. He had a savaged snout and no ears, none. Coons had chewed them off at the skull.

We got him not because he was wounded or finished, but

because he would not stay in a pen. He belonged to a tough old pulpwooder named Hoyt Cochran, who penned him with a gyp named Belle. But Joe was a climber, and so, when no one was looking, he would scale the chain link or dog wire like a monkey, and go hunt free. He did not run trash, and he was fearless, and he would hold a tree for five hours. "Hold a tree all night," my brother said. But a dog that cannot be kept is a worrisome thing, so Sam bought Joe cheap, probably saving him from a bullet.

He drove a steel rod in the dirt of the backyard, and fixed to that several feet of heavy chain. Joe lived most of his long life that way, staked down between his water bucket, food bowl—really an upside-down hubcap—and his doghouse, a plywood shell covered over with shingles and filled with fresh hay.

I would watch him there many days, my heart breaking a little, because nothing should live like that. Every now and then the wind would carry a scent to him there and he would drag his chain in the direction of that smell and pull it tight, his ruined nose twitching, and bay.

It came to me that his time on the chain was not living, and the only time he was really alive was on the mountain. There, he was something different. "He beat a lot of dogs, a lot of expensive, pure-breed dogs," Sam said, years later. To him, Joe was just one more discarded thing he was able to get some good out of, his way of saying to the discarders, yeah, the joke's on you.

Joe knew it, too, knew that he was something more. If he treed a coon with a pack of lesser dogs, or just one noisy dog who barked if he treed a coon or barked if he scratched himself, he would set himself apart, and fix his head in the direction of the coon and hold it there, as if to say to the humans, *If you were gonna bring along this white trash, what did you need me for?*

"He didn't like an ill dog," Sam said. "He meant for the others to behave."

He hunted him with a pure-breed black and tan named Blackie, a gift from an uncle. Blackie had a lovely voice but was prone to get lost, and wander for days.

But together, off in the distance, they made that beautiful sound.

Coon dogs have one bark when they strike a trail, an excited, insistent one, and another, steadier, melodic, as they trail, and a third, urgent, when they tree. But it was the trail bark that was most lovely.

"Joe had a kind of sharp *yerp* sound, and Blackie had more of a *yowl,* and when they were on that trail that sound would get to rolling, kinda, in the distance, and that was what was so pretty," my brother said.

———

Yerp!
Yowl!
Yerp!
Yowl!

And the boys in the cold and the dark forgot about falling off the mountain and slid and scrambled in the direction of that sound, faster and faster. It was the pure excitement of it that hurried them, not the chance that Joe would not stay treed. Sam knew that when he got there, there would be a coon either in the tree or dead on the ground, because if Joe caught one in the open, it was done. "He learned to kill them without gettin' hurt real bad, but not in time to save his ears."

This night, we were still what seemed a mile away when we heard that change—heard the baying ratchet itself up—and knew that the dogs were treed.

"Talk to 'im, son," my brother hollered, and the other little boys whooped, and I swear one or two of them jumped for joy. To say we didn't get out much did not nearly cover it.

We got there in time to see Joe running a wide circle around the tree, once, twice. The way he made sure that the coon had not outsmarted him, and slipped away. Then he put his front paws on the trunk, and sang to us. Our one good light played up into the branches of a pine, and there he was, a big boar coon. I know that a big boar was more than enough for most dogs, all teeth and razor blades. But he did not look big or dangerous. He just looked scared, behind his black mask, a thing I knew to be deceptive. Sam climbed the tree and, carefully, with a small ax, knocked the coon to the ground, and the dogs closed in. That might not be the way others did it, the purists of this sport, but it was the way a troop of bloodthirsty redneck boys did it in the winter of 1969. I do not remember a terrible fight, because Joe was such an assassin and was on his throat in an instant, but I remember an odd quiet when it was done, and boys, looking like little boys again, milling around, not sure what to do with their hands. We put the limp coon in the tow sack. There was a man in Jacksonville who paid cash money for it, not for the skin, but the meat.

My brother hunted another forty years, and still does, when his wore-out body will allow. He grew gentler—not a lot, but some—and sometimes just hunted to hear that sound, and dragged his dogs off the tree and went home once he knew the pretty part of it was done. He saw the sport change, and changed with it. He hunted on into his fifties, on into an age of tracking devices and shock collars. He carried a GPS. He asked me once to put the shock collar on so he could test it, but I have gotten some smarter since 1969.

But my time in the mountains, listening to the dogs, ended when I was a boy. When I think of it, which I often do, I am always ten years old, waddling across that mountain in so many pants my legs won't bend at the knee, knowing that if I fell I would never get up again.

Joe lived to be more than fifteen years old. "I finally just turned him loose," said my brother. "His teeth were wore down to nothing. But you know, I'd come home from work and he'd be gone, and I'd hear him off in the distance, and I'd have to go and get him off a tree, somewhere behind the house." It may be that there was a coon up there, or, near the end, it may be that he just thought there was. I guess there is no reason to think he would be any different from people, in that way.

Every now and then my big brother will ask me if I want to go for one last walk up the mountain, behind a new dog, but I just say, no, I'll listen from here. From the porch of my mother's house you can sometimes hear that sound, faintly, drifting down through the trees, and I shift my weight on the boards of the porch, and think how fine it is that an old man does not have to prove he is any kind of man, anymore.

A Word on Trash Talk

⁓

I AM NOT SUITED UP.

No one handed me a helmet, or diagrammed a play with me in mind. "Bragg up the middle" sounds like it would hurt a lot, and "Bragg sweeping around the end" would take much too long. I do not sweep; I stagger and, on a good day, plod.

No one has given me a pep talk for a long time, or even passed me a cup of Gatorade, though I am often thirsty. I am pretty sure, if I turn on ESPN, I will not be on the highlight reel, unless they have one for tackling biscuits and gravy.

Yet I am expected to do my part, this football season. I am to be a team player or I will be tied to the goalpost at Vanderbilt, and left to wither. Very rarely do they tear down the goalposts at Vanderbilt, so I would probably be up there a good while.

Actually, what I am supposed to do for the team does not involve doing anything. It involves *not* doing anything: not writing anything about anything that would make the opposing team mad, anything that football experts call, solemnly, "bulletin board material."

Sportscasters, perhaps hair-gelled into a state of confusion, believe this is a real thing, and that a fluttering scrap of newsprint thumbtacked to the wall in a locker room can be the difference between a National Championship and 0–13.

But even my friends believe in it, and have strongly hinted that I am sometimes a little bit of a smart aleck (though they did not really say "aleck") and sometimes a wiseacre (although they did not use the word "acre" either). In the past, in my enthusiasm, I have been accused of providing whole encyclopedias of bulletin board material. Well, no one can say that anymore.

My pen is dry, my voice stifled. I will not write that the football players at Ohio State, even the English majors, think Desdemona is a dandruff shampoo.

I will not write anything bad about Dabo Swinney, who has perhaps the best name in all of college athletics, and certainly not suggest that his dance looks a little like that gopher from the movie *Caddyshack*. I had a cousin named Dabo; he danced like a gopher, too.

I would never, ever write a bad word about Notre Dame, though my uncle did suggest once that the Irish only have to be half as good as any other team to get twice as much attention. But I would not write that, ever, because I do not want to receive mean e-mails from their imaginary girlfriends.

I will not write any of it. I am taking it for the team. I am on the bus.

I am glad Les Miles is still in coaching. I believe the national football landscape is better off with at least one coach who is about a half bubble off plumb.

And I am thrilled that Michigan is, as a team, spending spring break in Florida at a football camp, to recruit Southern athletes. Still, I bet their imaginary girlfriends get lonely, up there in the tundra. There is only so much ice fishing a body can endure.

The Superfan

~~⌒

I HEARD THAT ORBIE COOK HAD PASSED AWAY. Friday nights will be quieter now. Orbie was a fan of high school football and was famous for it, at least within the city limits of my hometown. In four decades under the lights, Orbie climbed into the stands to cheer on the home team. He was a big man to begin with, and when the kickoff tumbled through the night, he got bigger, louder, and somehow more precious to our people.

Funny that I knew so little about him outside the stadium, even in a town so small. But when I think of Friday nights, which are a little like church down here, I always think of the Orb.

It was the seventies, the first time I heard him. Then, a Friday began in the yard with a game of touch football inside the circle drive, until some knucklehead kicked the ball into the rosebushes. We were more than two miles from town, but I could hear the marching band tuning up, faint but clear. It was something by Chicago, maybe "Saturday in the Park," but I was pretty hopped-up on grape Kool-Aid back then and could be wrong.

Out on State 21, the marauders came, caravans of cars and big yellow school buses, cruising past the Rocket Drive-In and Roma's Pizza and Steak House. The soap on the car windows identified them as Yellow Jackets, Bearcats, and Valley Cubs, and they bore down on my alma mater with ill intent.

We had winning seasons . . . and losing seasons, but the Jacksonville Golden Eagles had the Orb. And the Orb was constant and—we thought—forever.

He was just a teenager then. He sat surrounded by his congregation, and I guess you could say he led cheers, though that does not come close to it. When the team, and the people, needed picking up, you'd hear that voice, echoed by the crowd:

"WE!"
"We!"
"WE DON'T!"
"We don't!"
"WE DON'T MESS!"
"We don't mess!"
"WE DON'T MESS AROUND!"
"Hey!"
"WE DON'T MESS AROUND!"
"Hey!"

He was still there after I graduated, and when I came back years later, a spectator again. By then, I'd figured out what Orbie was really about. It wasn't that he lifted the Eagles to victory. It was that he gave a booming voice to the joy of it, of being there, of belonging. The school gave him its lifetime achievement award, for spirit, before he died.

High school games are broadcast now on ESPN. I doubt if the bands play much Chicago anymore; I couldn't hear a tuba if it were in the laundry room.

Still, another season is on us. I think I will mix up some Kool-Aid. The doctor says I should avoid the sugar, but you can't toast a legend with Splenda—and, hey, I don't mess around.

Old Man and the Tee

⁓◡

I WILL NEVER FORGET the look of utter sadness on my big brother's face.

It was fall 2001. I had just opened the trunk of my car. You should never open the trunk of your car with witnesses standing nearby. There could be just about anything in there. "What's that?" he asked, pointing an accusing finger.

"They're golf clubs," I said in shame.

And something just broke between us. As teenage boys, we had done pick-and-shovel work beside a golf course in northeastern Alabama. We had stood, leaning on our shovel handles or against the hot hoods of my uncle's dump trucks, and made fun of the people wearing silly plaid or Day-Glo green, pink, and yellow clothes and hacking at little white balls like they were mad at them and then jumping into tiny clown cars and weaving off across the grass, usually drunk as Cooter Brown.

"Good ball!" they would shout whenever one of them hacked it into the short grass.

It did not look like something a serious man would do. And why would a grown man ever leave home dressed up like an Easter egg? Once, we saw a guy wearing knickers. Knickers. In Alabama. "Tallyho!" I shouted and laughed myself stupid.

But that day, with the evidence staring us in the face, my brother knew. I was a fraud.

I had tiptoed over to the other side, FootJoy shoes on my guilty feet and a putter in my hand.

What kind of man did anything with a putter? Say it out loud. Putter. Lord.

My brother never forgave me.

I stopped playing not long after that. I'd like to blame him for it, but the truth is, I quit because I was never going to be any good at it. I refused to take a lesson, believing that any chucklehead should be able to master such a ridiculous thing and thinking that would somehow keep my blue-collar pride intact. After losing nigh on five thousand balls and rapidly running out of friends who would tolerate me, I quit.

I gave away my shoes (which we, being cool, called "spikes") and my clubs ("sticks"). I had lost my last ball some months before. If you find one out there with "Callaway" written on it, it's mine. I guess you can keep it.

But now, in this season of renewal, I've decided it may be time to take it back up again. I've determined that, because I write for *Southern Living,* it may be time to become a gentleman. It's come down to golf or fly-fishing. The latter involves whipping a fishhook back and forth at your eyes. There are no sharp implements involved in golf—unless you sit on a tee. I have done this.

I think I will make my brother go with me. He retires this year, and I am afraid that if I do not find him a hobby, he will take to drink. He sold his bass boat, and his coon dog died.

I wonder if we can find us some knickers. Tallyho . . .

Fightin' Words

～♪

THINGS HAVE kind of gotten out of hand down here.

I love college football the way that some people love their dogs and children, but I have tried and tried to be civil about it, to be—no matter how old-fashioned and quaint this might sound—a gentleman.

But this is almost impossible to do in the football climate of today here in the South. Try to be a gentleman, and some guy with "Geaux Tigers" tattooed on his neck will slap the monocle off your face and attempt to strangle you with your own cravat.

When did it get to be this way? Don't we know that the dwindling football pretenders to the north—up in the icy wastelands of Ann Arbor and South Bend and wherever the heck Ohio State is—are staring hungrily to the south, lusting, envious, waiting for us to cannibalize ourselves?

Then, they will come roaring down on their snowmobiles and dogsleds and (because of our weakened state from playing genuine football teams week after week after week) strike while we are recovering from a night game in Death Valley.

We, as fans, have to do our part. We must build bridges and mend fences and—for you not-so-neighborly fans—stop throwing rocks at cars from out of state. We have to save up our behind-kicking frenzy for those teams from outside the South.

Of course, in a perfect world, the National Championship would not have to include anyone north of the Ohio River. Last year, it worked out beautifully as Alabama (Roll Tide) and Georgia battled in a truly epic game in Atlanta. It seemed like, for one gleaming moment, the outside world didn't exist. I did not even miss them. Well, maybe Wisconsin. Go Badgers.

But just in case someone outside the Southeastern Conference or the Atlantic Coast Conference should stagger, frostbitten, into the playoffs this year, let's cool it a bit when we play each other. Even our rhetoric needs to be toned down. At Alabama, at the end of games, the stadium roars: "Rammer Jammer, Yellow Hammer, Give 'em hell, Alabama!"

What if we just tweaked it a little and replaced the word "hell" with "smooches"? Say it out loud. Go ahead. See how nice that sounds? There is no need for cussing, anyway.

War Darn Eagle? See, it sounds almost as good.

At Mississippi State, do away with the abrasive cowbell. A harp would be nice. The Gator Chomp is unsettling. Just clap, like they do at the opera. Politely. The Arkansas Razorback is far too aggressive. Maybe it could be redrawn to look more like Porky Pig. I always liked Porky.

It's just a thought. I don't believe much will actually change. Some philistine of low breeding will likely hurl an empty bottle of Southern Comfort at the visiting team. Grown men will fight, though too drunkenly to do much harm. All I am suggesting is that we try.

Not long ago, at a Chevron station in Tuscaloosa, I watched a grown woman dog-cuss a cardboard cutout of Nick Saban in the window of the convenience store and then roar off in a big pickup truck. The tag read SPORTSMAN'S PARADISE.

Institutions

Above and Beyond

✦

THE LONGER I AM GONE FROM IT, the New Orleans I experienced as a young man seems more and more like a mirage, a shimmering, half-remembered thing, conjured not from shifting sands and searing heat but from humidity and hangover. Maybe nothing really looks the same, once the haze of dark rum or brown whiskey has burned off. I don't know. But the very best of it, the finest moment that I remember, happened in a hotel in which I never spent a night, never turned a key. It began, as I recall, at the bottom of a flight of dark, creaking steps, with loud laughter at my back and the sugary smell of Southern Comfort and candied cherries swirling thick around my head. The steps led, however improbably, into the very branches of the live oaks, into the air itself. And there, in the ancient trees that line lovely St. Charles Avenue, hung a strand of pearls. But that might just be the whiskey talkin'.

It could have happened anywhere, that perfect New Orleans moment.

I guess it *should* have happened at the Pontchartrain. I first came to this old city three decades ago, fell in love with it, and when I could not come up with a good reason to be here I came anyway, ultimately taking up a kind of semipermanent residence

in this historic hotel safely away from the drunken swill and bal-
lyhoo of the French Quarter. The bellmen kept some of my lug-
gage in a lobby closet; I was seldom gone more than a couple of
weeks, and knew that, unless I died from boredom in some gleaming metropolis of the modern South, I would come back to this city
within weeks if not days.

You had to see the Pontchartrain back then, see its frayed elegance and run your fingers over its gilded rot, to love it. It eventually faded out of business, and the Bayou Bar went dry, and the
piano man . . . well, I don't know what happened to him. I heard it
reopened, but that piano man had some age on him, and so much
time has passed, and . . . and so it will sound different this time.

There were a lot of perfect moments in the Pontch, but not *the*
one.

I always thought, in perhaps the best eating city in this world,
that the perfect moment would come on a plate, smelling of butter
and onions and garlic and cayenne, or on the half shell, or maybe
as a snowball in a paper cup.

No. Surely, then, it would come at a place like the one Celestine
Dunbar ran on Freret Street, before its walls vanished under a liquid nightmare. The best fried chicken and red beans I can recall,
the best stewed cabbage. People who think a vinyl tablecloth cannot be elegant never sat at her table. But as good and tragic as its
story was, it was not the moment, not *the* place.

Maybe, then, it was in the music. I watched Rosie Ledet mash
her squeeze box and make the entire clientele of the Rock 'n' Bowl
break into a cold sweat. Or maybe it would come not on a stage at
all but on Royal Street, in the hot sunshine, watching a young man
in a battered felt hat sing Sam Cooke for pocket change. Maybe.

I loved the place so much I even owned a house here, once,
there at the corner of Joseph and Annunciation Streets, Uptown.
I have said this before, but there is something remarkable about

waking up here. I would swing my feet from under the covers and, as my feet touched the hardwood floors of my shotgun double, I felt . . . well, I can't really explain. Like I could eat anything, drink anything, fight anyone, and get clean away with it. But life took me away. I still drive by there, and think of the good times, and wish I had stayed a quarter century instead of three scant years.

I'm just a tourist now. But once, I felt like something more. My moment came years before I ever owned even a teaspoon of the city. It was in the nineties, in a time when the crime rate was so remarkable, so achingly high, that it became its own culture. The wounded city, long before Katrina, staggered and danced back from that grave, too. It always does.

At the end of one bad day, I made plans to meet friends at the Columns Hotel on St. Charles, to have a snort of whiskey. But the place was jammed with after-work drinkers; it was like God opened up the courthouses and emptied every human with a good haircut and a Brooks Brothers charge card into this one hotel bar in one instant.

The Columns is a converted mansion, named for the massive columns in front, with a big front porch that I think rich people probably call a portico, but I have long since tired of trying to make them think I'm smart. The porch, too, was crowded, teeming. It is one of the things that set New Orleans apart. No matter how long or rotten your day, people will stand in tight shoes and high heels for two more hours, to bend an elbow with friends, and tell stories, and celebrate the very process of standing around and breathing air. It does not have to be Carnival. It can be the day the water bill comes.

But I needed a cove, a lee, a place away from the storm. On the second floor of the Columns is a balcony that rises above it all, a space reserved for the people who rent rooms at the hotel. But, somehow, we talked our way past the guardians of the stairwell and made our way up the groaning steps. I do not believe a bribe was ever even mentioned; I was willing to go as high as a twenty, for a quiet place to stare into a glass.

It was more than that.

I sank into a chair, into soft cushions. I cannot recall a word of what was said, only just being there. The live oaks swayed and creaked, up and down the avenue. I remember feeling the way I felt when I was a child, in the tree houses my big brother made. We fought Indians from there, repelled pirates. There's something safe and good about being up high.

You could hear the party downstairs, but muffled; you could smell the perfume, and the candied cherries and orange slices and lemon wedges, and cutting through everything the smell of whiskey and beer. But like the noise it was subdued, more like a memory of a thing, a ghost of it, and then the breeze took it away and replaced it with flowers.

I don't want to make too much of it; it was not profound, just peaceful. I don't think I've written that line much in my life. And then the streetcar, the clanking, whirring, beautiful, antiquated, inefficient, irreplaceable streetcar, broke through the settling dusk and the prevailing peace like a beloved, drunken, lurching uncle, and it just made things better somehow, because what is more New Orleans than that? The lights inside showed tourists, and tired ladies coming home from work, and young mothers battling with their children, and if I had not been so jaded I would have waved. I should have waved.

It left us there in the dusk, but there would be another, after a while, and another. It was then that I noticed the strand of white beads in the branches. During Carnival they call the big white strands "pearls," just plastic junk, but priceless in one fleeting second in time. The parades run right by here and I imagined some reveler in exuberance had flung them there.

I do not even know why I noticed. I had seen such a thing a hundred times. I guess it was just the moment. I am sure they have long since fallen to the sidewalk by now, onto the median, what the people here call the neutral ground. But it is nice to think they will sway there forever.

I do not think I lingered very long. It was just a moment, fine in itself. Most people have stories of New Orleans, brighter, louder, richer, raunchier, maybe even better.

I have not gone back to the balcony. But I think about it every time I ride down this beautiful avenue, in this great city, every time I see the tired ladies rumbling home from work on that steel streetcar, every time I glance overhead, to the trees, and see the broken and ragged jewels dangling above.

As I said, most people have a good bit more fun here than this.

June Is for Jellyfish

⁓

I CAME ACROSS A PHOTOGRAPH not long ago, in an album that all but fell apart in my hands. The faded color picture was taken more than fifty years ago with a Kodak Instamatic, and while the focus may have been less than pristine, the memory it jarred loose was sharp and clear. It showed an old woman and three little boys—my grandma, my brothers, and me—barefoot in the white sand somewhere near Panama City, Florida, on the dunes beside the blue-green Gulf of Mexico. I thought of a lot of things, good and fine and sadly sweet things. But mostly, I thought of stinging jellyfish and searing sunburn and stabbing stingrays and biting sand fleas and flip-flops that always wore blisters on my toes. And I thought about how I would like to meet that person who coined the cliché "It's a day at the beach" and punch him in the snoot.

The trip always began with great anticipation and joy. We could barely even catch our breath as we counted down the days, but that might have just been because we'd been blowing up floats and beach balls until we were blue in the face. It would have saved a lot of space if we'd just waited to do that at our destination, but it's hard to think straight when you're dancing on sunshine.

At the kitchen table, for weeks ahead of time, routes to the Gulf of Mexico were traced and retraced on maps—we still used maps then, made of real paper—and weather forecasts were scrutinized and perhaps even prayed over. Before we left home, the provisions were carefully prepared. Chickens were fried; coolers were filled with ice, cans of RC Cola, and half-gallon pickle jars of sweet tea; and brown-paper grocery sacks were stuffed with loaves of light bread, Bama mayonnaise, fresh tomatoes, and at least two bags of Golden Flake Cheese Curls (the first bag wouldn't make it past Montgomery, Alabama). The three-hundred-mile exodus took, it seemed like, an eternity. But finally—when our fingers and faces were all covered in orange dust—the tires of the old Chevrolet sank into the sand and we ran, whooping, straight into our misery.

We did not encounter bull sharks or barracudas or even undertows, for our Grandma Ava stood sentinel at the water's edge and shrieked if she saw a shadow in the waves or if we wandered out more than thigh-deep. But if there was a jellyfish, we brushed against it, and if there was a stingray, we accidentally stomped it, all the while soaking up the ultraviolence of the Florida sunshine until we glowed.

We flung ourselves onto the beach to recuperate, only to be consumed by pestilence, and then we fled back into the surf to try to drown them in the salt. Finally, at the end of the day, we staggered—blistered and almost paralyzed by the venoms of a half-dozen alien sea creatures—to the place where my mother and Aunt Juanita motioned to us from the white sand.

"Just ten more minutes?" my brothers and I pleaded.

I guess I've had ten more minutes now, a million times, a million jellyfish, a hundred stingrays, countless days of cruel sun. It seems like I would know better . . . by now.

Jubilee

⁓

HE CAN TRY TO TELL IT TO YOU, tell how the bay goes calm and slick just before dawn, how the tide pushes in beneath a gentle, easterly breeze that just smells different, smells like salt. He can tell how the mixing of water from the Gulf of Mexico and fresh water from the river delta to the north just fracture, somehow, in that great, warm, stagnant pool, and a heavier, saltier layer, low in oxygen, sinks to the bottom of Mobile Bay.

He can tell how the living things there, some of the best seafood in the world, feel that water go bad and seem to panic, and swarm to the shallows and even pile up on the brown sand of the Eastern Shore, tell how some old fishermen, who felt it all coming, will see the water writhe to life, and shout out a single word:

"Jubilee!"

He *can* tell it, can try to make you see it, but you have to be able to imagine, said Joey Gardner, who saw it the first time, he believes, in '63. People who can't imagine can't believe in such as this, not until they see it come writhing ashore with their own eyes. And even then, he said, "it's more like a dream."

"I was eleven, the first time," said Gardner, who has lived on the Eastern Shore of Mobile Bay since he was a boy. His grandmother warned him it was coming. It did every summer, at least once and sometimes two or three times, as the heat settled hard onto the Alabama coast and the water warmed to something like blood: "When the hurricane season comes, the jubilee comes . . . and that's when all the fish will come," the old woman told him. His grandma was a twin, he said, and twins just naturally know things like that.

But it would only last a little while, an hour, even less, and then the ecology of the bay would just right itself, heal itself, and that bounty of sea creatures, the ones not beached or gathered, would slip back into the safety of the brackish bay. The jubilee was like a gift, maybe even a blessing, the old people here liked to say, but you had to be quick to get your part of it. Late sleepers never, ever witnessed a jubilee.

He remembers the first time, how he woke to a great commotion in the usually quiet little city of Fairhope. People drove up and down the dark streets, shouting, mashing their car horns. Phones jangled. "Jubilee" was all the caller had to say, and then the phone would go dead, or be left swinging from the wall. People, half asleep and hastily dressed, hurried from the bungalows and cottages and old bayfront houses and down to the shore, bare-legged, flashlight beams bouncing in the dark. There were boatmen, and poets, and others who have always been compelled to live on the water, for reasons such as this.

"It was me and Johnny Miller, that first time; his momma treated me like a second son. He come up out of the dark when we were in the yard and said, 'So, you thought you'd slip off to the jubilee without me.' I sure miss Johnny. Cancer. He was a good friend to me," and he went quiet for a moment. The jubilee is how he marks time. "I remember I had a kerosene lamp, what they called a chromium lantern," like coal miners used to wear. He remembers how they chased its circle of light down to the bay, and played the beam across the shallows. The water, murky even in daylight, was teeming, alive.

"Now, imagine you're eleven years old . . ."

Flounder, some as big as hubcaps and in numbers beyond the counting, piled up like dinner plates in the shallows and up on the sand itself, flopping, wriggling, so many that you could gig three at a time. Eels tangled into a writhing mass, so thick that a man could not plant his feet to scoop them up in a five-gallon bucket. Catfish, thousands of them, seemed to be fighting not to stay in the water but escape it, only to be gathered up by old women and laughing children with nets or even pots and pans. There were shrimp, and rays, and other things that dwell on the bottom. But it was the crabs Gardner would never forget, "all of them just fightin' to get out of that bad water. On the seawall, the crabs were crawling over each other. You could see them pile up against the walls, like they were trying to climb that wall. They *were* trying to climb it. I thought it was The Judgment."

He is sixty-six now, and has seen many jubilees. He has been the herald himself, tipping off newcomers, sharing the secrets and the lore. Like so many people here, it has become part of him. "I had a chance once, to work for the railroad, to work on the L&N. But you know how it is when you're young. All you want to do is chase women." There was one young lady whose mother, when she learned he lived here, made him promise to call her when the jubilee came. And a man, of course, can't watch the water from a railyard. "I've been a carpenter, a plumber. I've worked a forklift, loading trucks, and on bulldozers. I worked at the paper mill." He never made it on the L&N, but, one or two mornings a year, a bucket in his hand, he is a great fisherman.

"When you're a kid here, you chase jubilees all summer," said Tony Lowery, a marine biologist who grew up on the bay, in Fairhope, and wrote his graduate thesis on the jubilee. "We slept on the wharf, and on the piers," waiting, watching for the early signs. "We'd see the eels coming in, sometimes, and see flounder on the surface, like they're trying to lift their heads out of the water." He and his friends gathered more flounder than they could carry, "cleaned 'em and put 'em in the freezer, and you have parties all summer, up and down the bay."

People who have lived here a long time said you could smell the flounder frying and crabs boiling for a mile or so. But it was never certain, never guaranteed. You could stare into the bay all night, all the conditions right, the timing perfect, and the wind would change, or it would fail to materialize for no apparent reason at all. It was the chance in it that made it fun, and has made that wonderment endure.

"Even a ripple" could ruin it, said Mac Walcott, an architect and fisherman here.

It happens in summer because that is when the bay is its most stagnant. The decomposing plants washed down from the deltas feed microorganisms in the bay, which explode in population and devour much more oxygen than usual. This, combined with the fracturing of the salt- and freshwater under the just-right weather and tide conditions, creates a heavy, salty, stifling environment. "Anything that can't float, that doesn't have a swim bladder," will try to escape that ecological trap, said Lowery. They have to swim to live. The strata of freshwater at the surface extends all the way to the shore, and draws them there.

The oxygen deprivation creates a kind of stupor, a languor. They seem to wait to be taken.

The jubilee is not an algae bloom, not like a red tide. There is no poison in it. It has been happening for as long as anyone can remember, and they know for a fact it was happening a damn sight before that. Civil War soldiers, scanning the bay for gunboats, watched it happen by torchlight, amazed. *The Mobile Daily Reg-*

ister told of the phenomenon in 1867, though it did not yet have a name. Once, before there were phones, and car horns, the old salts would see the bounty approaching, and ring a ship's bell. People speak of it here with a sense of propriety, sometimes a little mysteriously, even wondrous, but almost all of them remember how their grandparents handed them a bucket, or a shrimp net, and marched them down to the shallows, to glean. It was a little spooky, but it was also groceries.

"I grew up with an old black man—we called him 'The Duke'—and he taught me a lot of what I know" about the brackish water, and the nature of fish, said Jimbo Meador, a writer and fishing and nature guide, among other things, who has been wading the Eastern Shore and watching the changing nature of Mobile Bay for most of his seventy-eight years. "Daddy hired the Duke in the summer, mostly to take care of me. Made me my first cast net. We'd go out in a rowboat . . . and we watched that tide so close, it was right for a jubilee. And when we saw it we didn't holler damn 'Jubilee!' We didn't say nothin'. We gigged the flounder . . . gigged them in the head . . . and sold 'em to Mr. Stern at Stern's Fish Market."

His friend, Skip Jones, remembers a slightly more communal jubilee.

"My grandparents lived in a house on Point Clear, and I moved into that same house," said Jones, a builder, fisherman, and lover of old boats who has never lived very far from the water. Over the years, like Lowery, he learned what to watch for in the sky, on the surface of the bay. Whitecaps broke their hearts. The bay needed to look like glass. "You kind of just knew," he said, "and we'd go wake the neighbors."

The jubilee occurs regularly only two places in the world, say marine scientists and the people of the bay: It happens here, in places like Daphne and Fairhope and Point Clear and Mullet Point, and it is said to happen in the bay waters off Japan, which is so far away it might as well not count. No one here knows what they call it in Japanese, but they are pretty sure it is not "jubilee."

The first printed reference, by name, was in *The Register,* in 1912, when an old fisherman called the heaven-sent flounder and crabs a "jubilee." It just seemed to fit, somehow; such a thing, of course, had to have been pushed by the Hand of God. The name "jubilee" is derived from the Hebrew word for a trumpet made from a ram's horn; scripture refers to it as a kind of homecoming. In more modern times it has become shorthand for a season of celebration. In black churches in America, it is a reference to the heavenly reward, a time of joy.

It comes only in summer, mostly in August, usually once a year and may come two or three or more times, always on the rising tide, always before or at dawn, always when the weather is overcast or the morning after a light rain. Some swear by a full moon. The scope and the makeup of the jubilee can change, but rarely its duration. Often, as soon as word has spread, they are over.

"I been to crab jubilees, and flounder jubilees," said Gardner. Others seem to contain every bottom-feeder in the bay, including, sometimes, small sharks.

The jubilee is, as far as anyone can tell, mostly a natural thing, not triggered by pollution, though some people say overbuilding here, like everywhere on the Gulf Coast, may have some effect. It seems, some people say, like there are more of them, not less. Others say it is a warming Gulf and bay.

Some people might not see the wonder in it, but those people probably never spent five hours under an Alabama sun with a single line in the brackish water, praying for a croaker, or a speckled trout.

"As a kid, it was a phenomenon," said Skip Jones. "I mean, usually, we're just trying to catch a couple of crabs on a line baited with chicken gizzards. Then you get up in the morning and there's a zillion of 'em. All these creatures you worked so hard to get ahold of . . . then, on a jubilee, here would come some guy pulling a skiff along the sand, with five hundred flounder in it.

"I remember once there was a family of people who came through the yard and said, 'Is this a jubilee? Can we come?' And they waded out into the water but didn't have anything to put 'em in. I ended up giving them a bucket so they could empty the fish out of their pockets."

Landlubbers might be a little squeamish, at first.

"Imagine all this, in three or four inches of water," said Betsy Grant, who learned about the jubilee from Gardner, who promised to alert her when it occurred. She grew up in South Carolina but moved to the Mississippi Gulf Coast later in life, and then to Fairhope in 2011.

"It guess it was a little creepy. I got over that creepiness fast."

The crabs she saved for gumbo. The flounder she grilled whole, with just salt and pepper and a little olive oil. "Don't overcook it. It turns to mush," she said.

It is a natural thing. The people here do not feel guilty, or greedy. "I'm not going to leave fish to rot," she said.

It is so odd and wonderful and, well, distinctive that people here have named pretty much everything after the jubilees, from trailer parks to a cookbook from the Mobile Junior League. In the Fairhope area alone there is a locksmith, a glass cutter, three churches, a hardware store, a cleaning service, two dentists, a pet hospital, a paint and body shop, a photographer, a movie multiplex, and a pediatrician. There is Jubilee Print & Design, Jubilee Flooring & Decorating, Jubilee Auto and Marine Interiors, Jubilee Head Start, a car lot, and more, all named Jubilee.

It's so prevalent that some residents are reluctant to concede they have never actually seen one. Some might even lie about it, to belong, like pretending to vote Republican. Others are too ornery to care, like the author Sonny Brewer, who has written of life here, in novels and nonfiction, for some four decades.

"I myself have never seen one," said Brewer, who confesses he is not a good fisherman, in August or any other month. "Some people I trusted said they have, and I have eaten the fish. I guess it gives me something to look forward to."

But there is a rigid protocol to it all.

"I didn't cultivate my jubilee network," said Walcott. If someone calls, they expect to see you there, a bucket in hand. "If you don't respond, if you don't cultivate your sources, then the phone won't ring at four a.m."

Most places, that would seem a good thing. This is not them.

In the 1990s, said Walcott, a local radio station reported at about eight a.m. that there was a jubilee in Fairhope. "Traffic backed up for miles . . . for nothing. It was long gone. We called it the Radio Jubilee."

The people who have lived with jubilees all their lives stood beside the line of cars and shook their heads. Tourists. Landlubbers.

Walcott has his own favorite story of the jubilee, one of a young man who lives for them, waits for them, but never takes more than he can eat. He believes, Walcott wrote, "that fish should always swim ashore, and wait at men's feet."

My Affair with Tupperware

I USED TO WEAR TUPPERWARE ON MY HEAD. I thought it made me look like Spartacus. I'd sneak it back in the cabinet, and when I saw it again, it was full of peanut butter cookies. It seems like, sometimes, the best of life came in a plastic tub.

I try not to be one of those Southerners who waste whole days lamenting things that now lie discarded beside a road we'll never travel again. I try.

But I miss stadium hot dogs in wax paper. I miss real country music with steel guitar and soul. I miss old-growth forests in the shade of the stone mountains. I miss the white dunes of the Gulf, buried now under miles of concrete. I miss tea cakes, the kind my grandmother made. I miss the Amazing Rhythm Aces. I miss old barns telling me to SEE ROCK CITY.

I miss Tupperware.

Oh, I know there is still Tupperware out there, still enough stacked in the kitchen cabinets of this planet to make every boy with an ounce of imagination a plastic spaceman's helmet and another for his dog. I am sure, on a molecular level, new Tupperware is even superior to the container Earl Tupper invented in Leominster, Massachusetts, just after World War II. Plastic is forever.

It's the world that changed, outside that airtight seal.

It used to be, when you saw Tupperware coming, it was a celebration. Banana pudding arrived in Tupperware. Potato salad came in Tupperware. Cold fried chicken arrived in Tupperware, resting on a warm cloth. And when it was finally opened, the smell alone reminded you what a gift it was, to see another day. Tupperware meant reunions, dinner on the ground. Does cardboard elicit that, or a throwaway container from the supermarket?

If it came in Tupperware, it was worthy of such a vessel. You knew that, because on the lid of every bowl was written, in black felt-tip marker, the name of the chef who constructed that chocolate pudding crowned with Cool Whip. They fully expected to get that container back, and such precautions were required because every single piece of Tupperware seemed to be the exact same color of pale green. Tupperware was passed down, like crystal.

"It is the Wedgwood of the South," proclaimed my friend Randy Jones.

It even began life with a celebration. You did not just go buy Tupperware. You went to a Tupperware party, where I assumed there was drinking and poker and probably fistfights. I would learn, to my disappointment, there was rarely even a banjo. The woman who invented the Tupperware party, Brownie Wise of Kissimmee, Florida, did it as a marketing tool, and they spread even as far as Gadsden, Alabama.

"My momma was not the kind who went to a lot of parties," said Jones, who grew up in northeastern Alabama. "But she went to a Tupperware party."

My mother never went to one. "I heard they kinda went out of style," said the woman who serves her cranberry sauce every Thanksgiving in a fourteen-year-old margarine tub. Tupperware was just showing off.

I see it now and then at yard sales. Ten cents, usually. A quarter. It is hard for me not to pick it up, and put it on my head.

The Point of a Good Knife

$\sim$

ONE OF THESE DAYS, the last old man seated in the shade of the last country store on this earth will rummage around in the pocket of his frayed, baggy overalls and come out with a plug of Bloodhound, or Days Work, or Brown's Mule. He will not bite off a chew, for he is not a Philistine. He will rummage again, this time coming out with a bone-handled pocketknife of no more than three and no less than two blades, all so sharp he could shave a cat if he could get it to stand still, and cut off a chew. He will hold the knife a little longer than he needs to, run his thumb along the edge, maybe even open and close it a few times, one-handed, the way he saw the old men do it when he was a boy, sitting in this same shade, listening to them dog-cuss Herbert Hoover. Finally, he will snap it closed with that sharp *click,* with that sure, final sound a good knife has, and put it away for the last time.

Think, for just a moment, about your grandfather. He would have no more left the house without a pocketknife than without his breeches, for while a man of his era could survive this drafty world without pantaloons, he would sooner or later need to snip some twine, or punch a hole in an oil can, or dig a pine splinter out of some urchin's foot, or just slice an apple. One of these days, men will no longer love or need their pocketknives this way. That is when we know the last Southern man has shuffled off into the sunset, to make room for a world of helpless no-accounts.

I will never forget my first one. I would like to pretend it was a gleaming heirloom, handed down from the Yankee war, but it was just a busted, rusted wreck, with one-and-a-half blades, tossed into the bottom of a toolbox, forgotten. A single-bladed knife was useless; if it broke, you were helpless. Any more than three blades and you were a Swiss Boy Scout. This one, I reasoned, would have to do till I was rich and could afford a good knife, like a Case. I was maybe seven years old, but I put it in the pocket of my cutoff jeans and became, in that instant, a serious man. It was a German-made knife, its remaining blade and a half notched and pitted, but I was careless with it and it drew blood. Them German-mades sure hold an edge, the old men said when I showed them my sliced thumb, and told me my wound would most likely not be fatal, unless it got rust in it. I waited to die for much of 1966.

A Southern man, knifeless, was pitiful. Men without knives were like men who rode around without a jack, or a spare tire, just generally unprepared for life. A man without a knife could not fish, hunt, or work at any respectable employment. I am a writer, which is one step up from helpless, but I have always had a pocketknife. I believe, foolishly, it holds me close to my people.

In my hometown, some older gentlemen gather in the Huddle House to drink coffee and talk about the world as they know it. Not long ago, one of them walked over to my table and told me he enjoyed my stories about our world, and gave me a small, heavy box. Inside, wrapped in honest, oiled paper, was a perfect, three-bladed, bone-handled knife. It was a Case, a serious man's knife. I went in search of something to cut, and, this time, it was not me.

Old Florida Found

~⌒

W<small>E HAD JUST THREE NIGHTS</small> and four days in the Castaway Cottages, not near enough time in paradise if you consider the six-hundred-mile round trip to Panama City from northeast Alabama, getting lost twice in Montgomery, and the motoring power of a six-cylinder '62 Chevrolet Biscayne. By the time we got there, we were just turning around.

My mother, aunt, two brothers, grandma, cousin, and a dog named Barnabas all squeezed into a two-bedroom apartment with a pool in the parking lot and a black-and-white TV with a slow horizontal roll, and it was still about the most fun we ever had. We tumbled down dunes and got sand in our ears, and caught a crab in a bucket, and saw a dolphin, honest to God. We played miniature golf in a garden of cement dinosaurs, and would have had a beer-smoked hot dog at a joint called Lum's, but figured it was probably a sin.

But who would ever believe me up there in the red dirt where we started out, with just some cold fried chicken and tomato sandwiches and a frozen Clorox jug of drinking water? Who would believe these dunes and emerald water, if I couldn't bring a piece or two of Florida home with me? They would say I had just been to Leesburg, and got my glowing sunburn on the muddy Coosa backwater.

Then, on our last day, I stood in front of a giant, blinking sign that screamed SOUVENIRS!!! And I knew I was saved. The parking lot was so hot it stuck to the bottoms of my dime-store flip-flops, but looking back, it seemed as if I were about to enter Disney World, or what Disney World would be one day, when they drained enough swamp and got around to it. The store was as big as Walmart.

It was the summer of '69. I had a handful of damp white sand in one pocket of my cutoff jeans, clumped around a dozen perfect shells I culled from a million lesser ones on beautiful Panama City Beach. In the other pocket I had three wet, crumpled dollar bills, which meant I could afford almost anything in that place. They didn't mind at all that the money in my pockets was wet; the whole economy of coastal Florida would come tumbling down if they had to wait on money to dry.

I cannot remember the souvenir shop's name, but it was just like the one in Destin, and in Pensacola, and in Daytona, and in Cocoa Beach, and, well, any place where blue-green water and glimmering asphalt were held apart by hurricane-whipped palms, iridescent green putt-putt carpets, and restaurants that promised the best scampi or mullet or daiquiris in Florida. But I was ten years old then, and I didn't believe there was another place like it on this earth. I had not yet seen the rest of this dangling participle of a state, this wonderland, and to me this was Florida, a treasure trove of Budweiser beach towels, Styrofoam floats, leaky beach balls, and bottomless bowls of pinkie rings carved from abalone shell.

There were also hermit crabs painted with tiny flags, baby hammerheads and octopuses in bubbles of what seemed to be formaldehyde, and sand dollars, sea biscuits, and sharks' teeth strung on leather cords, the coolest things I had ever seen. There were puka shell chokers, ceramic dolphins mounted on clumps of coral, shellacked turtle shells, grapefruit spoons, chocolate-coated piña colada candy, Grateful Dead and Harley-Davidson do-rags, monkey heads carved out of coconuts, starfish, and an impressive array of conch shells, so you could always hear the Gulf of Mexico, even three hundred miles away. I could buy a miniature outhouse carved out of cedar, a desiccated piranha, an alligator foot key chain, a tiny Spanish galleon with matchstick masts, and a muscle shirt that identified me as LIFEGUARD, or CAPTAIN, or just BIKINI INSPECTOR.

But what grabbed me, what puzzled me, mostly, was a snow globe, in a place where the car hoods radiated enough heat on a summer day to send you to the emergency room. But I guess they were popular, because there was only one left. I picked it up and shook it, and watched the tiny plastic snowflakes drift down onto a tiny plastic beach with a single tiny plastic palm. And I thought how silly it was. That's not what Florida is. And I set it down and bought a shark's tooth on a string and a rubber alligator; that's what Florida is. I would spend a good lifetime discovering the rest, a kind of perpetual tourist in the state, on vacation even when I lived there, because the place just does that to you, somehow— just kind of frees you, even in a crawling traffic jam.

Maybe it's the palms, or the aquamarine water, or the sand, or how they all come together to make something that not even a century of concrete, climbing ever higher and wider, can ruin.

Oh, Old Florida took its hits. We used to eat good grilled amberjack and fried shrimp and stuffed crab at a place on Destin Harbor, till a hurricane wiped it from the landscape. In the reincarnation of the place, the hostess makes you swap your car keys for one of those blinking, buzzing pagers, as you wait in a perpetual line. It broke my heart, and it set me thinking about all that is gone and will never be again, and what is left and seems as if it always will be. I would like to see it all again, at least once, before I go off on a package tour to the Hereafter. Since I fear that will be someplace sparky and smoky, I think I would like to begin by bobbing in the water at least one more time.

I made my home in the best bobbing place on earth, as a young man, on skinny Anna Maria Island off of Bradenton and Sarasota, where you were only ever a block off the water in just about any direction. There, I lived on grouper sandwiches and piña coladas at the Sandbar Restaurant on the Gulf of Mexico. I remember pine needles in the white sand, and watching squadrons of brown pelicans hunt for fish in the flats of Tampa Bay. Nothing is prettier, at a distance; I've known people that way.

I used to take a swim every day at twilight in the turquoise water near Bean Point, and watched it fade slowly into an inky dark pool. I was told the bull sharks fed at dusk, so I hid among a senior citizens' exercise group. I am not proud of it, but now that I am old enough not to stand out quite so much, I would do it again if I had a chance. On the weekends I fished the same flats the pelicans did, and watched a hammerhead as long as the boat glide underneath, in water as clear as a mountain spring and three feet deep. I could see myself living there forever, see myself as an old man in a chair under a palm tree, how he would one day think he might retire soon, though that might just mean changing chairs.

Maybe, someday, I will do that, still.

Miami left a different impression. There, I always kind of felt that, if I ever stopped moving, a civil uprising from a conflict across the sea would just pull me into it, somehow, and I would be seen waving a placard or maybe a pistol. I don't know; maybe it was just the Cuban coffee. I lived there for years and always felt like I was on the edge of something else, something greater and maybe just a bit dangerous, a weird and pleasant unease, if such a thing is possible. A hunk of concrete hit me in the head there one day, but the closest I ever came to dying was when I consumed too many *croquetas de jamón.*

I was there when Hurricane Andrew blew in, in a little house in Coconut Grove; I rolled up in a futon to ride it out, with a café con leche and a Cuban sandwich and a bag full of Haitian macaroons. On a second tour of Miami I bought a house in Coral Gables, not far from the iconic Biltmore Hotel; I saw a crab, once, backstroking through the swimming pool, and I went to have lunch under an explosion of orchids to think about it.

I remember driving across the Glades and counting alligators, just lined up there, dozing; remember falling out of the boat on an alligator hunt in Lake Okeechobee on a night thick with raindrops and mosquitoes and glowing, orange eyes. I remember going to do a story on the saltwater crocodiles at Turkey Point, and seeing one, a massive female, beside the boat, big enough to eat that hammerhead in Tampa Bay, if she was inclined. I held a baby one in my hand; it felt like a boot.

I remember it was the last time I had a cat, a stray who lurked for lizards in the banyan trees, and I remember thinking how he could not have lived anywhere else; he was specific to this place.

I remember a burning Haitian rum called Barbancourt, but I do not remember it very well. And I remember bribing the front man at Joe's Stone Crab, or trying to, till I realized that a twenty-dollar bill will not get you a seat one damn bit sooner. I got old, waiting on a plate of those claws.

But mostly I remember how I could go get some black beans and rice and *tres leches* at Versailles restaurant, and listen to people for whom revolution was not a feeling, but a memory. It may be I am too old for South Florida now, too old to stand on the edge of anything, lest I lose my balance and tumble off. Still, I go back every chance I get, tempting fate, one *croqueta* at a time.

Maybe I should stick to the west coast, where there seemed to be fewer high rollers. I sat on a dock most of one afternoon off Siesta Key, next to a one-eyed dolphin. I think his name was Sam. Then I went in and got me some stone crabs, and I do not believe I bribed a soul. I'd like to go back there, but I reckon Sam is gone.

One memory rides easy, even easier than most. I was working down on Anna Maria in . . . well, I cannot recall, around '91 or so, and a cold wave had penetrated deep into the state, killing the orange trees. I had to call my mother and tell her I would not be home for the holidays. The interstate was iced over, as far down as southern Georgia. I was, quite truly, marooned on an island.

The temperature dropped freakishly low, and I walked out to the beach, with nothing better to do. And I saw snow falling on the white sand, and on the fronds of a palm tree, and into the Gulf of Mexico, and I stood there a long time, shivering.

I remember thinking that, even after so much time, I still didn't know what Florida was.

I guess I still don't, but if I ever see another snow globe like that again, I will buy it, and set it on a shelf. You never know where this life will lead you, and one day it may lead me far, far from a beach.

Jerry Lee and Me

THE BIG CAT'S DEAD, glass eyes glared up from the floor.

"That's Jane," the rock-and-roll singer said from his comfortable chair.

The cat, a mountain lion, had been reduced to a tawny rug on the floor of the den, and now snarled, silently, from beneath the big black grand piano. The rock-and-roll singer had named it—the rug, not the piano—for his second wife, a hellish woman who was hard on a windshield, who went at him and his vehicles with Coke bottles, and claw hammers, and flying Santa Claus figurines.

"Knocked me down the stairs one time," he said.

He thought on that awhile.

But then, a lot of women did.

"One time, this woman hit me right in the forehead with the pointy heel . . . Atlanta . . . I believe it was the seventies . . . Blood went ever'where . . . Had to stitch me up. . . ."

I asked him if he deserved it.

He tried to recall, but it was lost, somewhere.

"I'm sure I did . . . for somethin' . . . somebody. . . ."

He nodded at the dead eyes of the lion.

"Ain't that right, Jane?"

Of course, it was going to be a long, strange trip. I knew that when I picked up the phone, about three years ago.

New York was on the line. Little stuff never rolls down from New York; that city does not do piddling. It is my imagination, surely, but I'd swear that receiver felt warm in my hand.

"Do you have any interest in doing a book on Jerry Lee Lewis?" my agent asked.

A cautious man, a deliberate man, would have carefully considered this, and gone and hid under the bed.

He learned the piano in his hometown of Ferriday, Louisiana, but Memphis had been the launch of his stardom, there under the nicotine-stained acoustic tiles at Sun Studio. He still lives just a few minutes down Interstate 55, down the Delta, not far from the big river in northern Mississippi. He was born in the bottomland. It is where he will end. On the way to his house, I passed a dead armadillo; armadillos die ugly. I had read somewhere, in one of the million or so stories told about him, that he was haunted by armadillos, which are said to feed in the low-country graves. But people say a lot of things, believe a lot of things, when a man's legend swells beyond the scope of normal people and normal things, as if everything about a man has to have some degree of dark magic in it, even roadkill.

It was hot that first afternoon, hot for all the weeks to come, as if the dog days had settled hard on DeSoto County and stuck like flies on the lid of a jelly jar. The big iron gates—the ones with a piano on them—swung open from the middle, creaking and shuddering like something from a scary movie. I drove up to the big brick ranch-style house, built on the edge of a man-made lake. I had interviewed a million people, but not a legend before, not the living history of rock and roll, not one of the last true troubadours.

"A driving blues shouter . . . taking off like wildfire . . . phenomenal," lauded *Billboard,* in its Pop, Country & Western, and Rhythm & Blues sections in 1957. Writer Jim Jerome called his voice "a laser of grief" in *People* in 1978. In *Esquire* in 1982, Mark Humphrey wrote: "If you think a redneck can't sing the blues, just listen to him belt out 'Big Legged Woman,' or 'Sick and Tired.' If you think he's always a snide bastard without a redeeming trace of sincerity, listen to his moving rendition of the gospel standard 'Will the Circle Be Unbroken.' And if you think anything about the man can be neatly pigeonholed, think again." The words themselves were not often poetry, but poetry is hard to dance to. It is how you sing it, pound it, that matters, or you might as well read it off a post office bulletin board or the bathroom wall. People called it genius, and he became a man you made exceptions for, to hear him do his thing.

In his hometown, in a rambling museum crammed with memorabilia, I knew, there was one of the many grand pianos he had played over a career that spanned six decades or more. He rarely walked in a room with a piano he did not, at some point, take over by divine right. Even Elvis, the first time they met, surrendered the piano to him. Still, visitors to the museum ask. Did Jerry Lee play that one, that very one? And his sister Frankie Jean, the curator of the museum, just sighs. "Well, I guess he did," she tells them. "He played every one in the world." But wrapped around the genius, weaving through it, was such death and suffering as to be medieval. What was left of him? I wondered as I opened my car door.

I was set upon by a small pack of dogs, each one a different breed from the other. I was reassured by the people who looked after the man that they did not usually bite—well, all but one. His name was Topaz, Jr., and he was about the size of a squirrel monkey. His sire, Topaz, was an old dog and lay near death, and Jerry Lee Lewis grieved. Like a lot of people who have left a certain amount of human carnage in their wake, his heart broke over a dog, or over an animal of any kind. His friends love to tell of the time he saw a donkey painted to look like a zebra down in a Mexican border town, and, pretty well drunk, wanted to put it in the car and take it home with him to Memphis, take it away from all the craziness, fireworks, and tequila. He was not altogether convinced it wasn't a zebra, but whether it was or not his friends talked him out of it, though that donkey/zebra stayed on his mind a good long time.

I knocked on his bedroom door, reinforced by iron bars. He lay there in the gloom, bullet holes in the walls, a rummage sale of memories stacked on the shelves and on the walls; there would have been more, but the IRS had raided him across the years. Hank Williams, his photograph draped with a black ribbon as if the man in the bed was still in mourning, looked down on me from the edge of a chifforobe. The man himself, even in pain from a half-dozen ailments, was still handsome, his hair still thick and wavy but silver now, no longer that burnished gold that had made even the church ladies feel a little funny during "Great Speckled Bird."

"Never did see him . . . play for him," he said of Williams, and it seemed so odd to hear regret in that man's voice that I actually wrote the word—REGRET?—in big letters on my legal pad. He did just about everything else in his life he ever wanted to do, did some of it almost perfectly, most of it wildly and with feeling, and some of it . . . well, he had a good time in the chaos, doing that, too. He was only seventy-seven then, but seventy-seven for Jerry Lee Lewis is like being seventy-seven in dog years. Still, all the pills and whiskey and needles and more, from all those nights on and off stage, had only laid him up, not put him down. The jealous husbands had not left a mark on him, after so much time.

"I'm still here," he told me, as if reading my mind.

"Yes, sir," I told him.

But they've had your obit written, I thought, for quite some time.

He is done with all the mess now; he is immersed in clean and righteous living. He is still Jerry Lee Lewis, though, not able to leap to the lid of his grand piano but still able to make it ring with honky-tonk, blues, gospel, all the genres he had helped weld into rock and roll, so long ago, when the music rose up from a little storefront studio on Union Avenue and swept like a storm across the country and the wider world. He had conjured that, him and Elvis and the great Chuck Berry and the rest, and he is not done yet. He is still recording; his last two CDs were his best-selling collections, ever. Bruce Springsteen sang backup on "Pink Cadillac." Think about it. Like I said, it can be tricky, with legends.

I have been doing this stuff a pretty good while, taking people's memories, making something from them that is more than just a window dressing of life. I have come to believe it is best to just talk awhile across some common ground. But music is his life and I am no expert; I could not play a comb and tissue paper, and in second grade had been asked to hand in my kazoo. But we both loved our mothers, me and him. He would even change the words of his songs, to sing about it. One song had haunted me, one he did in the Memphis years. I could not talk the Yankee editor into putting it in the book, but it almost made me cry.

> *Can you really rock and roll, Billy Boy, Billy Boy?*
> *Can you really rock and roll, charming Billy?*
> *Yes I can really rock and roll, I can even do the stroll*
> *But I'm a young cat, and I can't leave my mother.*

So we began with that, with the woman who brought him cocoa and vanilla wafers for breakfast in bed, but, when he fell hard from grace and fame, had been a steel rod driven through him and into the earth itself. He could not have lain down and died, quit, if he wanted, not with that woman standing there to remind him he was her blood, too. And so we talked about mommas, and biscuits, and sometimes the ringing, stinging flat of their hands. People said his momma was ashamed he played the Devil's music, "but that was bull," he said, hotly. His momma sat alone as her hard-drinking husband served time for bootlegging, survived the death of a precious child, dragged a cotton sack. What would have shamed her, he said, was to accept defeat in a time when people were saying such mean things about her boy. Once we got that straight, the rest was easier. Sometimes a romantic notion is just that, a theme. It was hard to bind together a theme in his life, like trying to take a thousand lightning bugs dancing in a field, and mash them together in one beam of light. But I know he meant it, when he talked of loving her.

I know because, as my own mother lay on an operating room gurney in Alabama, as I fretted in the waiting room with my big brother as a surgeon put a stent in her heart, my phone rang. It was the Killer speaking.

"How is your mother?" he asked.

I told him she had been so tired, lately.

"Well, you tell her it might not be her heart," he said. Sometimes, he said, it can be hard to carry around all those years.

"Jerry Lee Lewis asked about you, and wished you well," I told her later, in recovery, but she was on some pretty good drugs right then, and I could have told her it was John the Baptist's head. Still, it meant a lot to me.

Over the weeks we talked about heaven, and hell, how he was trapped between a religion that was preached so awful hard, and a life of temptation so dark, so delicious, a superman could hardly resist. Most people have to choose, here in the South; they just don't have quite so much to pray away. As the weeks went by, he told me stories about honky-tonk fights and pharmaceuticals and passed-out airplane pilots, and shooting false teeth off the wall of a dentist's office. He rarely got mad at me even when I had to ask him some harsh questions, questions about his drug use, his women; and I had to ask mind-breaking ones, about the coffins that had passed him by, including those of two sons. I had read he once shot a bass player, more or less accidentally. One afternoon, he showed me a brushed-steel .357, but he was not mad at me at the time and, me being a Southern boy myself, I think he thought I would just enjoy seeing it, the way other people might show off a Matisse, or a Ming vase. He kept it under a pillow, "in case somebody bothers me," he said, and smiled at me. I smiled back, but on the way out the door I realized he had not meant to shoot the bass player, either, and he had bled all over the white shag carpeting.

He was not in good health when we began, and would, over the next few years, swing close to death more than once, with pneumonia and shattered bones threatening him, and arthritis causing him unrelenting pain, and I was, frankly, afraid my book might be written after he—probably snarling like that rug—left this world. But that was old hat, for Jerry Lee. Doctors had told him, to his face, that he was going to die, to prepare himself for his Maker, and that was before he got old. In two years' time, from when we began the interviews, he was not only recording again but playing in Europe.

Once, thinking about death, he raised his hands to his face and spread the fingers out.

Time has not touched them at all.

Spooky.

At the end of the day, as we neared completion of the interviews, his wife, Judith, would give me some good iced tea in a Tupperware glass, in a kitchen that smelled of cooking vegetables, potatoes and green beans, and stew. Judith had been married to his cousin and ex-wife Myra's brother, and if that seems somehow complicated to you, you have obviously not followed his life at all. Jimmy Swaggart is his double first cousin; his bass player—the one he did not shoot—was his cousin and father-in-law. It gets better.

Most people know some of it, how his daddy, Elmo, mortgaged the farm to buy the boy a piano, and how he beat it like it stole somethin', beat it with pure genius, mixing the music of the Assembly of God with juke-joint blues and hillbilly music and everything; how he went to Sam Phillips—the man who found Elvis—and rode rock-and-roll music to the moon, man, music like "Whole Lotta Shakin' Goin' On." They have heard how Elvis, drafted into the army, went to Jerry Lee and surrendered his crown, and wept. "I's gonna take it anyway," Jerry Lee said. But then his marriage to his thirteen-year-old cousin, Myra, blew up all over the newspapers, and he fell, on fire, into mean little beer joints and no-tell motels, playing some big dates, still, but not like it was. But he refused to vanish, and played and played, because if you have a talent like his you do not leave it staked down in the yard like some forgotten dog, and in the 1970s he went pure, hard country, and made more money than Standard Oil. He partied himself to the edge of death, two times, three times, more. Along the way, he crashed a hundred Cadillacs, a dozen Corvettes, flipped a Rolls-Royce or two, and rammed the gate at Graceland going to see his buddy, not intending any harm, just misgauging the length of a Lincoln Continental's front end. People threw their hands in the air and squealed that he had come to kill the King. "Ridiculous," he growled.

It does puzzle him, how that mystery train rolled on and on. One of his keepsakes is the black-and-white photograph *Million-Dollar Quartet,* taken when Johnny Cash, Carl Perkins, Elvis Presley, and a still relatively unknown Jerry Lee Lewis came together at Sun Studio in Memphis on December 4, 1956. It shows four young men gathered around a piano, singing songs from the radio, from their childhood, and from church. But only Elvis and Jerry Lee, raised in the Assembly of God, lingered for long after the picture was taken. "Johnny and Carl didn't really know the words . . . they was Baptists," he said, and therefore deprived. He and Elvis sat on the bench together, singing, talking into the afternoon. They were good friends, once, bound by a common delight, of being part of a thing so glorious as rock and roll, and by a common dread, whether or not a man can play rock music and not be consumed, in the end, in a lake of fire.

That photograph of the four young men would become one of the iconic images of American music, and a source of great irony. "If you'd asked one of us, asked anybody, 'Who's gonna be the first of all of us to die?' the answer would've been, 'It's gonna be Jerry Lee Lewis,'" he said.

Now there is only him to speak of the creation, only him, with wheelchair-bound Little Richard and a frail Chuck Berry and reclusive Fats Domino, to shout of the birth of rock and roll. "Daddy took after Chuck one time with a barlow knife," he said, never claiming memory is a neat and tidy thing. He fought Carl Perkins across the trunk of a '57 Buick. He watched Johnny Cash steal a motel TV.

"We was legends," he said of those early days. "We was legends, an' we didn't even know it."

I would forget that, sometimes, sitting next to the man's bed, him talking about how they haven't made a good car since the '59 Cadillac, or of pulling corn with his daddy, or his momma's tomato gravy. I would forget that the words "shake it, baby, shake it" are enshrined in the Library of Congress, that his music is honored in museums and halls of fame. The Beatles, the Rolling Stones, and other legendary performers say he, as much as anyone, lit the fire and showed the way. Some days, he seemed like just a good ol' boy, a man you could tell a story to. And you laugh and laugh, because you know that no matter how outrageous a thing is that you might have done, he did it, better or worse, and did more of it, and if he can do all that for all these many years and still be breathing—no, living—then there is hope for all the rest of us. Surely we will live forever.

Old Men Behaving Badly

~⁀

SOMEONE SHOULD HAVE WARNED ME about that third Lucky Dog.

Someone should have saved me from myself in that long-ago Carnival, on that crumbling street corner. They should have just slapped it out of my hand and driven me back to the old Pontchartrain Hotel for a bicarbonate and an intervention.

But sometimes people just don't show good sense when the big floats start to roll down lovely St. Charles Avenue or through the teeming Quarter. They forget their finer natures, and sometimes pants.

When I was a boy, I loved stories of Carnival in New Orleans, loved pictures in the history books of the elaborate floats lit by throngs of flambeaux carriers, the costumes of the revelers cut and pieced from another time. You could almost hear the music coming off the page.

I could not wait to see it, till I heard the marching bands and stood in a shower of beads.

There is nothing like it, people told me. Go to Zulu, they said. Snag a coconut. Discard your dignity and scream, "Throw me something, mister!" Enjoy the unbridled excess of Fat Tuesday, and wake up, morbidly hungover and dehydrated, and get smudged on Ash Wednesday.

217

"But I am not Catholic," I said.

They told me it was a little like Saint Patrick's Day. "Everyone's Irish?" I said. Yup, they said. But they should have warned me about . . . stuff. They should have told me about beads. They should have told me that thirty-two floats will pass you by and not one soul will even look your way, because as a grown, somewhat nondescript man, you are far down the list of targets. You rank behind all women of all kinds, all grandpas on stepladders with catch nets and knee-high compression socks, all children, all men in Dr. Seuss hats (because you could not get snockered enough for a Dr. Seuss hat, even if you had not grown up Congregational Holiness), and tree limbs. Live oaks will catch more beads than you.

Then, at the precise moment that you have given up, the instant you stop paying attention, someone will slap you in the face with a six-foot string of artificial pearls manufactured in Malaysia for thirteen dollars a ton, or almost put your eye out with a shower of purple aluminum doubloons. And the odd thing is, you'll be grateful. You'll out-leap a sweet lady on a Rascal scooter for a plastic cup.

Flip-Flop Weather

IT IS WINTERTIME. Yesterday, it was a bone-numbing 47 de-grees. I think I even saw a mosquito, though he was wearing a jacket and a little bitty pair of pants.

Oh, will spring never come? Down here, we all try to cope with the cold. My brother Sam cuts and stacks wood for the fireplaces, stockpiling for the winter, one in which we will huddle around a single, sad sparkler and a flickering Zippo lighter. We have enough wood to heat Albania. He goes into the wilderness in insulated coveralls and thermal boots; by eleven a.m., he is nicely broiled.

My mother believes, too, this will be a winter that never ends, and has been known to shelter in place, eyes locked on the weather forecasters in Birmingham, warning me of hard freezes that seldom come and snow that rarely falls.

"Call in sick," Momma says if the mercury plummets below 72. I look out on a balmy day. "You don't need to travel in that," she says.

Me, I like winter. I turn the thermostat down to something approximating a good draft, wrap up in an old blanket, and turn on the television to watch the weather. I don't take any joy in human suffering, but there is just something satisfying about reclining down here in the artificial chill, the only ice around tinkling in your glass of tea, as you watch snowplows labor and snow tires spin in the miserable tundra to the far north. I lived a few winters in Boston and New York; there are no words for the horror.

Now I just sit in my chair and watch ruddy-faced people tug on the cords of their snowblowers, and I sigh. Maybe, I think to myself, if it slips below 80, I shall make a pot of chili.

We used to have winter. I do not mean a hard freeze for three days, or an ice storm, but days of cold. If you are a Southerner living aboveground—as opposed to hunkered in a hole living on cans of Beanee Weenee—you must admit that the weather has changed. Those winters of my childhood are now lost in a haze of growing humidity, swallowed up by the milling throngs of Southerners wearing camouflage Bermuda shorts and Taylor Swift tank tops, moaning through Walmart in a mild sweat, shopping for Velveeta and Ro-Tel tomatoes. There's no celebrating a football national championship without cheese dip.

Oh, I know they still have winter in the snowy peaks of North Carolina, up near Lake Superior, but in the states below, it seems, not so much anymore.

I remember waiting for the big yellow bus, stamping my feet to stave off frostbite. I remember the hot air of the heater on my toes, and gazing out on a world glinting with frost. I remember how my brothers and I skated across it in our shoes, falling, falling, falling some more.

Now ice is a hated thing. It slicks the interstates a few days a year. It freezes and bursts the pipes on a Tuesday; by Wednesday night, people are in flip-flops. It is not a season but an aberration.

Better to wait it out like Momma, I guess, and remember ponds of silver and hope that, up there in the tundra, they get that snowblower cranked.

Thrill of the Hunt

~⁀◡

M Y MOTHER SHELTERS IN PLACE in February. She thinks
that if she can hole up for twenty-eight days, she will survive
the bone-chilling harshness of an Alabama winter till the buttercups push their way out into the glory of spring. Leap year is, in
her eyes, just mean.

I try to lure her outside with treats, kind of like we used to do
with a beloved old dog, Gizzard. But unlike Gizzard, who would
run through a wall at the mere possibility of a scrap of bologna,
she's not easily bamboozled.

"How about we go get us some catfish?" I ask.

"Hon," she says, "they're saying on Channel 6 that it might
snow."

Not unless God Himself floats over and sprays us with a can of
starch, I think.

Only one thing will get her out of her comfortable chair, there
beside the glowing fireplace. "Wanna hit the thrift store?" I ask.

The next sound you'll hear will be the banging of the screened
door, loud as a pistol shot.

She'll be sitting in the passenger seat, buckled in, by the time I
find the car keys.

My family loves going to the thrift store, and we frequent about fourteen of them on a regular basis. I guess we're afraid we'll miss something. Life does not change much from day to day at the mall; what they have on a Tuesday, they'll have on Wednesday. But every day at a thrift store is a whole, big, new world of possibility. It all depends on whim, on chance—or, as Momma says, "what the rich people get tired of."

I started going to them because my mother, no matter how much her life has changed, will always be a child of the Depression, a survivor of the foothills of the Appalachians. Dollar General, to her, might as well be Saks Fifth Avenue.

In the thrift store, she can buy a pair of khakis for two dollars, more or less. She can find a nice jacket for three dollars. She is loyal to the stores in northeastern Alabama but admits there is a special thrill in the ones on the Gulf Coast.

"Them rich folks," she explained, "throw away some nice stuff."

She used to like a good antiques/junk store, too, till last year. She got tired as she was perusing the long rows of an antiques mall in Daphne, Alabama, and sat in a chair with a DO NOT SIT sign, which was obviously meant for other people.

As I circled back to her minutes later, I saw her motioning to me, almost frantic. "Ricky," she whispered, "that man over there is starin' at me."

"Who?" I asked.

"That man," she said, pointing. There was no one there, except a life-size terra-cotta statue of a Chinese soldier.

"How long has he been lookin' at you?" I asked.

"Since I sat down," she said. The cataract surgery might not have been as successful as we had hoped.

So, in this slowly dying winter, we will stick to the thrift store. The selection may not be as good, but at least we know the coatrack is unlikely to flirt with her and the shoe bin will not ask for her phone number.

Living the Southern Dream

⁓

I WAS BORN IN RED MUD, hemmed in by cotton poison and johnsongrass, across a rusty pasture fence and down the shimmering blacktop from a clear-cut mountain. My first textbook on Southern history described slavery as an inconvenience. I grew up in a time of Wally Butts, Boone's Farm, Molly Hatchet, Merle Haggard, and *Walking Tall*. As a young man I left it, left for a good while, then came home to stay, to get old in the thick air and descend, in time, into my ancestral soil. I have found my South just as troubled and imperfect as ever. If anything, the mosquitoes and nitwits are winning.

I have always known this South is not idyllic; it will break your heart. But the good in it, the best of it, held us fast, even if we could only go home in a dream, to a dream, to houses hewed from heart pine and decorated with a lace of dogwoods, the kitchens smelling of the best food on earth. It even had its own magazine, this finer, gentler South. It came to us stacked in a cardboard box, faded, torn, dog-eared, with rectangular holes where the coconut cake used to be.

We never got a new *Southern Living* when I was a boy; relatives and friends would send them to us, sandwiched between yellowed *Constitution* newspapers, a few *Sports Illustrated* magazines with

Frazier and Ali on the covers, and a stack of sports pages from the Sunday *Birmingham News,* syrup rings encircling the scores of games played a season gone. I didn't care that they were out of date, those copies of *Southern Living.* I read about eggnog in August, and cooling cucumber concoctions as the water pipes froze three feet underground.

I will not lie and pretend I read with interest insights on gazebo architecture. I was in elementary school and did not greatly care about how I could construct a koi pond. But I would in time come to see the magazine as an oasis. It was not a society sheet; its writers told, instead, of a life we might one day live, when we caught our breath, when we got a little bit ahead. Women like my mother found in its pages an escape, just as surely as if they had scaled a chain-link fence. I would hear, in time, even the rich ladies saw it that way. It came every month in the mail, like a file in a birthday cake.

Me, I consumed the stories on food. It is a wonder I did not actually tear out and eat the first picture of a bone-in rib roast I ever saw. Much of the time, the accompanying recipes had been cut away, but that did not bother us. My mother never looked at a recipe; God Himself whispered the ingredients into her ear. But for the less blessed, these stories and photos were a promise, a raising of the quality of life one breakfast casserole at a time. They showed me a wider world, a richer one, as close as next door.

The fact that I would one day grow up to write for it is as big a surprise to me as anybody else, proof that you can, if you can get him to stand still, sprinkle perfume on a hog. I fit inside these pages because I write about Momma, and mudholes, and tides and Tupperware. I guess I will continue, until they raise their standards. I have gotten used to reading it, unsnipped.

Alabama Road Trips

⁓

MY GRANDFATHER heard the song of the blacktop all his life. Charlie Bundrum knew other melodies. He heard the whisper of the river, and knew that if he followed that sound it would lead him, drifting, beneath the willow trees that lined the Tallapoosa, or to the slow undulations of the water moccasins who swam in the brown Coosa. He knew that if he followed it far enough, as far as the great dam on the Tennessee, the water pooled so deep it was almost blue, and a man could catch catfish as big as a grown hog.

He knew the singing of the rails. He would run alongside the lumbering freight cars that plied the Alabama-Georgia line, and catch a free ride to Birmingham or Mobile or Muscle Shoals, a tow sack full of hoop cheese, canned salmon, and saltine crackers swinging from his belt. The railroad bulls did not frighten him. He carried a roofing hatchet in his belt, to open, he said, his "Co'Colas."

But mostly, when he went looking for something special, he followed the blacktop. From the open window of his raggedy Model A Ford—or any other old car he had managed to flag down from the johnsongrass at the side of the road—he watched his state, his Alabama, roll slowly by, corner to corner and bottom to top, from the autumn of the highlands to the blue-green waters of the Gulf.

He often sang as he traveled, sang "Boil Them Cabbage Down" and "My Bucket's Got a Hole in It" and everything Jimmie Rodgers ever made, and he would have played the radio if he had ever owned one. It was the Depression then, when life seemed in shades of gray, but not his Alabama.

Even in the grip of such awful sadness, it shined.

He took my mother and her sisters with him, sometimes, when they were still children, every bigger girl riding with a smaller girl on her lap, the children passing crackers and tins of potted meat back and forth, till the babies were in such an awful mess. Along the way he pointed to houses he had worked on, in the better times.

"I built that," he would say, as if it was a palace. And he would sing about buying a pistol as long as he was tall, and about shooting some poor woman named Thelma, "just to see her jump and fall."

"Where we goin', Daddy?" one of the girls would eventually wonder.

And sometimes he knew the answer to that and sometimes he only knew when they got there, when some river glinted through the pines, or some lake shimmered ahead, or some strange man came lumbering out of his mountain shack, a jar of clear liquor in one hand, or sometimes just a greasy paper sack full of chicken backs and cold biscuits. "Git out," he would offer, but usually they just talked through the window.

He did not call them road trips, at least not that any of his children can recall. He called it loafering, and sometimes just "visitin'," and since he knew everybody in the known universe, he may well have been telling the truth.

My grandma just called it gone.

My father heard it, too, the music in that asphalt. He followed it not to something but away from things, and I guess every woman or man decides that when they turn the key.

For him, his chariot was a prewar Mercury with a perfect paint job and an engine that had worn out not long after VA Day. It looked fine sitting in the yard but on the road it belched black smoke like a locomotive, and backfired so violently that people in his hometown of Jacksonville wondered if perhaps someone might be robbing the First National. He carried five-gallon jugs of burnt motor oil with him, sloshing in the trunk, till, inevitably, the old pile of rolling junk died at the side of the road. Then it was a Hudson Hornet, something slick and fine, and he drove it as fast as it would go with my mother hanging on to whatever she could grab in the passenger seat, drove it all around the world, from Hokes Bluff to Dripping Rock.

He drove with one elbow out the window, serenaded by the clinking of what might have been Coke bottles rolling around in the back floorboards but probably were not. He had come home from the mean cold of Korea with a restlessness in him that seemed to ease only when he was rolling, so he rolled as long as there was money for gas. He watched cotton mill baseball games from Alexander City to Leesburg, gigged frogs in Cleburne County, and, far to the south, stood over Hank Williams's grave.

But mostly, he liked the sweep of the rivers, liked to just sit and look at them with his bare feet poking through the door, "Young Love" playing on the radio until the battery was stone-cold dead, and he had to beg some stranger to jump him off.

He took me with him, sometimes, when I was barely old enough to see over the edge of the door, and we joke now, in my family, that because of this I knew every bootlegger from Rome, Georgia, to the Mississippi line. But sometimes his late-night trips were an act of mercy. I had trouble breathing as a toddler, and sometimes it seemed the only way I could catch my breath was through the open window of that car.

Sometimes it still seems that way.

―――

It was inevitable, I guess, I would hear the same music they heard, in the singing of tires.

By the time I was sixteen, I knew what the road was for. A road was not just some avenue that linked you with the feed store, or the Piggly Wiggly, or the Dairy Queen. The Alabama roads were freedom, at least till your car broke down. And who's to say that you were not right where you were meant to be, when it did.

When I was sixteen, I rode a '66 Corvair so far into the deep green of northeastern Alabama that I was greatly surprised to learn I had been in the frightening, alien state of Georgia for the better part of the evening, and had little or no idea how to find my way home again. They didn't even keep the right time, in Georgia. Who knows what barbaric things might befall me, before I crossed over into God's country again? I had no reason to go, no purpose, other than what I now know is called wanderlust, which is a little like finding out the name of a disease that has plagued your family since the beginnings of time.

When I was seventeen, I rode the length of the state to the coast, for spring break. I only took one class that year at Jacksonville State, but I believed I was a scholar. I made the trip with a lovely young woman who sang in the choir in the Baptist Church in Saks. I remember cool sand and colder water, and something delicious they called a deviled crab. And then the week was done and we came home. Charlie, I think, would have stayed. Daddy might have never come home.

When I was eighteen, I rode a 1971 Camaro—gold with a white

racing stripe—into the infield at Talladega, not so much to see the race but to witness the bacchanalia that was said to go on there. The Camaro had a short in the electric system and had to be pushed off every time we turned off the ignition, but it still had a racing stripe. I don't know who won the race at Talladega, but now I do know what bacchanalia means.

When I was nineteen I rode a Triumph Spitfire up Cheaha Mountain to see the view and eat supper, a fine, romantic evening till a buzzard the size of a Piper Cub hit the windshield on the way down. The worst of it was trying to find parts for a Triumph Spitfire in Jacksonville, Alabama, in 1979.

But at every turn, at every long straightaway, across what is now becoming a long life, I have loved the roads of this state, and the places they take you. I have loved every pork chop biscuit bought in every gas station in every town not big enough for a café, loved every hot fudge cake, loved every foot-long hot dog that ever ruined a shirt. The roads have been my balm, and in many ways my education. It may be that I am just romantic, and cannot recall the potholes at all. That does not mean I will stop traveling anytime soon.

EPILOGUE

Expatriates, Exiles,
and Southerners at Heart

~⌇

I GET A LETTER almost every few days from an exile, or expa-
triate, from some lost Southerner who dreams of home. It's not
that they are unhappy where they are, only that they slip, now
and then, into their idea of home, an idea polished by distance,
or time.

They usually begin with something like: "I am standing with my
feet frozen to the sidewalk in Pittsburgh, and . . ." I understand it,
because I have been frozen to many sidewalks, myself.

Once, I think I might have actually died, but it turns out I was
just in Utah.

But now and then I get a note from someone who was not born
here, but who feels, somehow, perfectly at home, who leans over
an oyster po'boy in Uptown and decides to take the old, clanking
streetcar back to their hotel on Canal Street, because it just takes
longer.

These are the people who think they can still hear cannon on
Lookout Mountain, and can quote whole lines from *The Prince of
Tides* when they see a shrimp boat's nets, like wings, flying above
the grass as it threads through the low country of marsh and mud.

These are the people with a conch shell, still roaring like an
angry ocean after all these years, but now gathering dust on a

shelf in East St. Louis, and people with a family recipe for butter-milk pie, three generations old, slowly fading away on a refrigerator door in Queens.

They are the old, playing an immaculate album of the great Hank Williams on a bitter-cold night in Boston, and the young, dancing like there is no tomorrow to a nuevo-redneck rocker in a hip Manhattan bar, saying how, man, if they could just get to Nashville. . . .

They may come here all the time, or they may never get South again, but they will walk through Memphis with Elvis and Jerry Lee, and wander the Delta with Muddy, and wave, languidly, to a waiter in the Monteleone, with Tennessee.

I see a lot of cabdrivers. We slide through the snow, together, and they always, always hear my accent, and always, always say: "You know, I was down there one time, and . . ." and they all have a story, about a song they heard or a girl they knew or a thing they ate, and off we go, the tires sliding on the ice, the horns blaring, the muffled curses bouncing off the glass.

"Been meaning to go back," they always say.

And then there are the few who have never been.

"Well," they always say, "I did once fly through Atlanta."

Acknowledgments

A collection like this requires more work than you might think, some of it beyond my skill. For that, I would like to thank Nicholas Thomson, Jennifer Simpson, Hannah Dugger, and the good people at *Southern Living* and *Garden & Gun*.

I am grateful, as always, to Amanda Urban and Jordan Pavlin, for staying with me despite myself, and to my family, for the same.

Attributions

"The Outcast" was published in *Garden & Gun,* June/July 2017.

"You Ain't Goin' Nowhere" was published in *Southern Living,* January 2019.

"This Means War" was published in *Southern Living,* June 2019.

"The Mean Season" was published in *Southern Living,* August 2019.

"The Heat Monster" was published in *Southern Living,* August 2015.

"Life in the Slow Lane" was published in *Southern Living,* May 2018.

"They Must Be Mad" was published in *Southern Living,* February 2019.

"Dear Grumpy Gardener" was published in *Southern Living,* July 2017.

"The Great Conroy" was published in *Southern Living,* May 2016.

"The Talker" was published in *Southern Living,* April 2018.

"Harper Lee" was published in *Garden & Gun's S Is for Southern,* May 3, 2018.

"Spirit of the Mockingbird" was published in *Southern Living,* April 2016.

"The Best of Who We Are" was published in *Southern Living,* October 2017.

"The Dancing Skinny" was published in *Garden & Gun,* August/September 2019.

"Return of the Goat Man" was published in *Southern Living,* March 2016.

"The Picture Taker" was published in *The Picture Taker: Photographs by Ken Elkins,* 2015.

"Keeping It Real" was published in *Southern Living,* July 2019.

"There's a Tear in My Beer" was published in *Southern Living,* January 2016.

"Hot Chicken Is So Not Cool" was published in *Southern Living,* August 2016.

"The Chariots of My People" was published in *Southern Living,* January 2017.

"The Abominable Biscuit" was published in *Southern Living,* September 2015.

"Dangerous Games" was published in *Southern Living,* July 2018.

"Driving Me Crazy" was published in *Southern Living,* April 2019.

"Hands Off My Sandwich" was published in *Southern Living,* August 2017.

"Let's Eat Pig's Feet" was published in *Southern Living,* April 2017.

"Home of the Po'Boy" was published in *Garden & Gun,* October/November 2011.

"Don't Mess with the Recipe" was published in *Southern Living,* March 2019.

"Savor the Bread Pudding Soufflé at Commander's Palace" was published in *Garden & Gun,* April/May 2017.

"Why Nothing Beats a Classic Southern Diner" was published in *Southern Living,* January 2020.

"Later, Gator" was published in *Southern Living,* March 2020.

"Fishing for the Moon" was published in *Southern Living,* March 2017.

"Why Momma Loves Me Anyway" was published in *Southern Living,* May 2017.

"Along for the Ride" was published in *Southern Living,* June 2017.

"Kitchen-Sink Curls" was published in *Southern Living,* August 2018.

"Mariachi Momma" was published in *Southern Living,* June 2016.

"Who's in Charge Here?" was published in *Southern Living,* May 2019.

"Why I Write About Home" was published in *Longleaf,* Summer 2009.

"I Ain't Scared of You" was published in *Southern Living,* October 2018.

"Free Spirits" was published in *Southern Living,* October 2019.

"The Ghost of Halloweens Past" was published in *Southern Living,* October 2016.

"Praise the Gourd" was published in *Southern Living,* October 2017.

"A Homespun Ghost Story" was published in *Southern Living,* October 2015.

"Planes, Trains, and Turkeys" was published in *Southern Living,* November 2015.

"Socks, Underwear, and a Camaro" was published in *Southern Living,* December 2016.

"The Canned Stuff" was published in *Southern Living,* November 2017.

"Dear Santa (Again)" was published in *Southern Living,* December 2015.

"I Beg Your Pardon" was published in *Southern Living,* November 2018.

"The Christmas Kid" was published in *Southern Living,* December 2017.

"Bah, Humbug!" was published in *Southern Living,* December 2018.

"Better Watch Out" was published in *Southern Living,* December 2019.

"A Hard Bargain" was published in *Southern Living,* November 2019.

"Can I Get an Amen?" was published in *Southern Living,* November 2016.

"Burying the Bear" was published in *Southern Living,* September 2019.

"The Sweetest Sound" was published in *Garden & Gun,* December 2013/January 2014.

"A Word on Trash Talk" was published in *Southern Living,* September 2016.

"The Superfan" was published in *Southern Living,* September 2017.

"Old Man and the Tee" was published in *Southern Living,* March 2018.

"Fightin' Words" was published in *Southern Living,* September 2018.

"Above and Beyond" was published in *Garden & Gun,* February/March 2016.

"June Is for Jellyfish" was published in *Southern Living,* June 2018.

"Jubilee" was published in *Southern Living,* July 2019.

"My Affair with Tupperware" was published in *Southern Living,* July 2015.

"The Point of a Good Knife" was published in *Southern Living,* July 2016.

"Old Florida Found" was published in *Garden & Gun,* December 2019/ January 2020.

"Jerry Lee and Me" was published in *Garden & Gun,* October/November 2014.

"Old Men Behaving Badly" was published in *Southern Living,* February 2017.

"Flip-Flop Weather" was published in *Southern Living,* January 2018.

"Thrill of the Hunt" was published in *Southern Living,* February 2018.

"Living the Southern Dream" was published in *Southern Living,* February 2016.

Foreword from *Alabama Road Trips,* by Alabama Media Group, was published June 2014.

A NOTE ABOUT THE AUTHOR

Rick Bragg is the author of more than eight books, including the best-selling *Ava's Man* and *All Over but the Shoutin'*. He is also a regular contributor to *Garden & Gun* magazine. He lives in Alabama.

A NOTE ON THE TYPE

This book was set in Charter, a typeface designed at Bitstream by Matthew Carter in 1987. Charter is a revival of eighteenth-century Roman type forms.

Composed by North Market Street Graphics, Lancaster, Pennsylvania

Printed and bound by Berryville Graphics, Berryville, Virginia

Designed by Maggie Hinders